True Happiness

Can Be Yours

Presented To:

_____

Presented By:

_____

Contact Me At:

_____

_____

_____

_____

True Happiness Can Be Yours

ISBN 0-9704497-0-4

E-Mail Address:
book@densu.com

Internet Address:
http://www.densu.com

True Happiness Can Be Yours

Chapter One

True Happiness is something we all desire and seek to obtain. No matter what our nationality, race, age, gender, social status, intelligence, religion or education, we all want to experience and enjoy True Happiness.

The fact that we share a universal desire to obtain and experience True Happiness tells us that it is something that should be an integral part of our daily lives and that each of us is justified and right in his or her search or quest for True Happiness.

The entire world system is always attempting to provide us with anything and everything that might bring us True Happiness, but if we are honest about the quality of our lives, we have to admit that we are not truly happy; something is still missing!

The authors of this book believe that every person, no matter who he or she is, is entitled to and meant to have a truly happy life, and therefore, we now share with you:

True Happiness <u>CAN</u> Be Yours.......

In the beginning, God created the heavens and the earth. All was good. The earth was a wonderful paradise where He placed the first man and woman after creating them in His own image and likeness.

They lived a wonderfully blessed life as they reigned together with their Creator. God gave them power and dominion over all living creatures on the earth and told them to be fruitful, multiply, fill the earth, and subdue it. God basically placed them in charge of everything down to the naming of the animals.

The Garden of Eden, which was their home, was a paradise. The word "Eden" actually means pleasure and delight. They had constant fellowship and communion with their Creator and harmony with His creation. There was no sin, no violence, no sickness or disease, no lack or want of any kind, and no death. This was God's plan for all people and still is today!

Adam, the first man, and Eve, his wife, had the most wonderful life that anyone has ever had on earth, and this was also God's plan for the entire human race -- all who would be born of Adam and Eve. They had an abundance of everything to make them truly happy, but to protect their happiness, God placed one restriction on them.

"You are free to eat from any tree in the garden; but you must not eat from the tree of the knowledge of good and evil, for when you eat of it you will surely die."

God gave Adam and Eve the ability to choose. He did not create them as puppets or robots. He desired a relationship with them based on mutual trust and respect. God did not want them to die and told them to not eat from that one tree. They didn't trust God and were deceived as follows:

Now the serpent was more crafty than any of the wild animals the LORD God had made. He said to the woman, "Did God really say, 'You must not eat from any tree in the garden'?" The woman said to the serpent, "We may eat fruit from the trees in the garden, but God did say, 'You must not eat fruit from the tree that is in the middle of the garden, and you must not touch it, or you will die.'"

"You will not surely die," the serpent said to the woman. "For God knows that when you eat of it your eyes will be opened, and you will be like God, knowing good and evil." When the woman saw that the fruit of the tree was good for food and pleasing to the eye, and also desirable for gaining wisdom, she took some and ate it. She also gave some to her husband, who was with her, and he ate it.

Then the eyes of both of them were opened, and they realized they were naked; so they sewed fig leaves together and made coverings for themselves. Then the man and his wife heard the sound of the LORD God as he was walking in the garden in the cool of the day, and they hid from the LORD God among the trees of the garden. But the LORD God called to the man, "Where are you?"

He answered, "I heard you in the garden, and I was afraid because I was naked; so I hid." And He said, "Who told you that you were naked? Have you eaten from the tree that I commanded you not to eat from?" The man said, "The woman you put here with me—she gave me some fruit from the tree, and I ate it." Then the LORD God said to the woman, "What is this you have done?" The woman said, "The serpent deceived me, and I ate."

The consequences of Adam and Eve's choice to not trust their Creator, to ·not take Him at His Word, were devastating to the entire human race, both then and now. Adam and Eve's unbelief and disobedience brought sin into the world and alienated mankind from their Creator. All forms of evil and selfishness, along with sickness, disease, and even death, followed their disbelief and sin.

Adam and Eve, the parents of the human race, chose to believe the serpent, the devil, Satan, instead of believing their Creator God. Not only was mankind alienated from God by sin, but Satan now had dominion on earth among the human race. Adam and Eve had been given authority by God over all earthly creatures including the serpent, but by obeying the devil instead of asserting their authority over him, they became slaves to sin and Satan instead of ruling and reigning with God, their Creator.

Life on earth for them and for all mankind was no longer what God had originally intended. Living became an existence rather than a life filled with God's blessings and abundance. The entry of sin into the world, resulting in man's separation from God and the rise in Satanic activity on earth today, help us to understand why the human race is in such a state of chaos, confusion, and turmoil and why people are experiencing such a low standard of life, with all the selfishness, sickness and disease, poverty, suicide, murder, sexual sin and perversion, rebellion against authority, divorce, drug and alcohol abuse, and all the other evils of society.

Out of ignorance, and by the devil's own design, most people blame God, or "the gods" for the chaotic condition of the world today and for the problems they face in their own life, family, and country. Not understanding what the real problem is, and without any real solutions that work, mankind fights to survive and get ahead and even succeeds at life, only to find that in the end, they face death, the judgment, and eternity without God.

People everywhere go through the motions of life everyday trying to find something that will fill that void in them but without success. Entertainment, worldly amusements, sex, drugs, alcohol, sports, careers, relationships, even religion, fail to fill that God-shaped void that only a relationship with their Creator can fill. Satan and his world system give pleasure for a season, but it is short lived and in the end, brings even more pain and emptiness.

God, in whose image and likeness we were all created, continued to value and love mankind, even though people had been separated from Him by sin and disbelief. Even though His love for us had not changed, our Creator could not violate the rules He had made about the consequences of sin, or His Word would then not be trustworthy. Therefore, He had to implement a remedy to solve mankind's dilemma so that He could again have fellowship with us and restore us to our original state of peace, blessing, and abundance, as well as our God-given authority on earth while upholding the truthfulness and integrity of His Word.

God's justice had to be satisfied. Mankind's sin and disobedience had to be punished. The punishment for sin was death, not only the cessation of our bodily life but also our spiritual death, which is separation from God. This is the reason why people who die in sin go to hell and are separated from God's presence forever, even though hell was originally a place prepared for the devil and his fallen angels.

However, instead of destroying the entire human race, God provided a way for mankind to be saved from their sin and reconciled with their Creator so it could have fellowship with God and life as God had always intended. He made a way to redeem us, to buy us back from the slave market of sin, and also from Satan's control over our lives. God accomplished this through His Son, Jesus Christ.

For God so loved the world, that He gave His only begotten Son, that whosoever believes in Him should not perish, but have everlasting life. God's Son, Jesus, was born supernaturally in the city of Bethlehem, in Israel. A virgin girl named Mary was the mother of God's Son, Jesus. The Holy Spirit of God overshadowed Mary, causing her to conceive and bring forth the Holy Child of God, Jesus.

All of this had been predicted for centuries before His birth, as was Jesus's purpose for coming to earth and the other events that would take place in His life. All prophecies about Him were fulfilled down to even the smallest detail. He grew in favor with God and man, living thirty-three years here on earth and fulfilling His purpose for coming, after which He returned to His Father in Heaven.

Jesus was different than any other man. He had no earthly father. He was not of Adam's bloodline. God was His Father, and although He was tempted by Satan, as Adam and Eve were in the beginning, Jesus never sinned. He overcame every scheme and every temptation of the devil. He always did the will of God and lived in complete obedience to His Heavenly Father.

Therefore, Jesus Christ was able to fulfill God's plan for redeeming mankind. He was God's solution to our problem. Instead of punishing us for our sins, God punished His Son, Jesus, in our place. Jesus

Christ, the only perfect, sinless human being to ever walk this earth, sacrificed His life for you, me, and the entire human race. Jesus Christ was nailed to a cross, died over 2,000 years ago and shed His precious blood in payment for our sins, to redeem us from sin and its effects, and from Satan's control over our lives.

Jesus Christ became our substitute. He suffered our punishment on that Cross. **Jesus, who had no sin, became sin for us, so that we might become the righteousness of God in Him.** He traded places with us. He became who we were so that we could become who He is. He bore our sins, sickness, and disease in His own body on that Cross and gave us His righteousness, health, and abundant life in its place. He took our defeat and gave us His victory. He died so that we could live life abundantly as God had originally intended.

Jesus Christ died for our sins as was prophesied. He was buried, and then He was raised on the third day, also according to what was foretold about Him. He then appeared to Peter and the other disciples, and then to more than five hundred of His followers at the same time. Shortly thereafter, Jesus Christ ascended into Heaven where He is now preparing a place for all who choose to believe in Him and receive Him as their Savior and Lord. Someday, Jesus will return to bring to Heaven forever all those who believe in Him.

Jesus Christ has conquered sin, sickness, disease, death, and all the works of the devil. He is alive and reigns victorious now and forever. He did this all for you, me, and the entire human race; and for whoever comes to Him and trusts Him, and puts his or her faith in His shed blood and receive Him as their own personal Savior and Lord. **Whosoever calls upon the Name of the Lord will be saved.**

Everything in this book is based on Truth as recorded in God's Word, the Bible. The Bible is God's written record, account, and revelation of Himself to mankind. God has preserved His Word for thousands of years so that you and I can know what to believe, how we can be saved from our sins, and how we can be redeemed, restored, and reconciled to God, our Creator, our Savior, and our Friend.

You have now read the Good News about Jesus Christ, that He died on that Cross over two thousand years ago in your place, and for your sins as your substitute to bring you back to God. He suffered your punishment and torment, so that you would not have to go to hell when you die and suffer everlasting punishment. Your sin caused a debt that you could not repay. He paid that debt for you in full. It cost Him His very life to redeem you, and He did it all to prove His love for you. You are loved by God!

How will you respond to God's love as you consider the fact that He gave His one and only Son to die in your place so He could bring you back to Himself? And how will you respond to Jesus's love for you, that He was willing to die in your place and suffer your punishment so you could have Eternal Life? And how will you respond to the Holy Spirit, Who is revealing Jesus to you right now? How will you respond? You have two choices!

You can respond in faith and believe the Gospel, or you can respond with disbelief, rejecting the Good News about Jesus. You can accept the precious gift of God's Son He paid for with His very life, or you can do nothing and thereby reject Him and all that He offers you. You can receive God's forgiveness and be reconciled to your Creator, or you can remain dead in your sins forever. You can call on the Name of the Lord and be saved, or you can continue to be lost without God and without hope.

God wants you to trust Him and to receive His Son Jesus and all the resulting benefits, but Satan wants you to doubt God like Adam and Eve did in the beginning and remain as you are under his control. God wants you to be blessed. Satan wants you to be cursed. God wants to help you. Satan wants to hurt you. God wants you to live free from the effects of sin. Satan wants you to live in bondage to sin. God wants you to live in abundance and divine health. Satan wants you to live in lack and sickness. God is the author of life. Satan is the author of death. God wants you to enjoy Heaven forever with Him. Satan wants you to be tortured in Hell forever with him.

Jesus Christ went about doing good and healing all that were oppressed by the devil. He healed the sick, made the blind to see, the deaf to hear, and the dumb to speak. He cast out evil spirits, He raised the dead, healed the lepers, and made the lame to walk. He healed everyone that came to him in faith, no matter how serious their sickness or disease. He forgave the sins of everyone that put their trust in Him. **Jesus Christ came into this world to save sinners, and He was manifested to destroy the works of the devil.**

Jesus Christ is alive forevermore, and is the same yesterday, today and forever. The works that He did 2,000 years ago, He still does today. You can trust Jesus. His love is real. **All the promises of God are "yes" and "Amen" in Jesus.** When Jesus said, **"I am the way, the truth and the life; no one comes to the Father, except by Me"**, He meant just that. There is no other way back to God, except through faith in Jesus Christ. Jesus said, **"I am the resurrection, and the life: he that believes in Me, though he were dead, yet shall he live: And whosoever lives and believes in Me shall never die."**

The Bible says, "But as many as received Him (Jesus), to them gave He power to become the children of God, even to them that believe on His Name". The Bible also says, "That if you confess with your mouth, "Jesus is Lord," and believe in your heart that God raised Him from the dead, you will be saved." It is also written, "Everyone who calls on the name of the Lord will be saved."

Now it is time for you to make a choice, the most important decision you will ever make in your life. You did not arrive at this place and time by accident. God's love has brought you to this point. His Holy Spirit is drawing you to Him so that you can be saved and have a whole new life -- a life of peace, joy, security, happiness, and abundance -- and the promise of life everlasting in Heaven.

If your choice is to remain as you are under the control of Satan, you should go back and reread this chapter and prayerfully consider your choice. If you want to be restored to your Creator and live the life He originally intended for you with all its benefits, you can say the following prayer right now:

Dear God,

Thank you for creating me in Your Image and Likeness and for not giving up on me, for valuing me and loving me so much that you gave your Only Begotten Son, Jesus Christ, to die in my place to buy me back from the bondage of sin, and out from under the control of Satan, all through the shed blood of Jesus Christ.

I, here and now, choose to believe in the Name of Jesus Christ, and I open the door of my heart and receive Jesus into my life, as my Savior, my Healer, my Deliverer, my Redeemer and my Provider. With my mouth, I confess Jesus Christ as Lord and believe in my heart that You have raised Him from the dead. I believe that Jesus is alive and that He is the same yesterday, today, and forever. I call on the Name of the Lord to be saved right now!

Thank you for saving me and for forgiving and forgetting all my sins. I am changing how I think and feel, and because of Your love for me, I purpose in my heart to live a life of love towards You and others. I believe You are the only True God. You are now Number One in my life. From this moment forward, I want to know You and do Your Will, instead of living my life apart from You as I have in the past. I renounce Satan and everything and anything that exalts itself against the knowledge of You and Your Word.

Thank you for accepting me just as I am, for making me your child, and for giving me an entirely new and abundant life full of all your blessings, just as if I had never sinned. Thank you for being my Heavenly Father and for the gift of Eternal Life. Your love, forgiveness, and acceptance are beyond my comprehension, but I receive them all with a very grateful and humble heart, and I look forward to growing in my relationship with You and discovering who I am as Your child.

I will no longer doubt either Your Existence, or Your Word. I believe that You are Who You say You are, I believe that You do everything that You promise to do, and I believe that You have done for me everything that You say You have done for me. I also believe that I now am who You say that I am, and that I have what You say that I now have, and I believe that I now can do everything that You say I can.

Therefore, I take my new and rightful place in Your family as Your child. I am thankful for my new life and ready to live as You know is best for me. Heavenly Father, please fill me with Your Holy Spirit, teach me Your ways, and guide and direct my life completely, as I love You and trust You to guide me into all Truth. Help me to always know what pleases You, and then give me the boldness to do it. I really do want to please You.

Jesus, thank You for bearing my sins, sicknesses, and pains in Your body on the cross, and for taking the punishment that I deserved for my sins. The shedding of Your blood and your other acts of love for me make me want to live for You and honor You with my life. I am thankful that You now live in me, that You are here to stay, and that You will never go away. I believe in You, Jesus. AMEN!

Record Of My Decision

Let it be known to all in Heaven, on earth, and under the earth, that I have received Jesus Christ as the Savior and Lord of my life. In my heart I believe that God has raised Him from the dead, and with my mouth I confess Him as Lord.

Name: _____

Date: _____

Time: _____

Place: _____

Please write and tell us about your decision, so
we can rejoice with you and pray for you:

DenSu Ministries
Box 26393
Akron, OH 44319 USA

True Happiness
Is Now Yours

Chapter Two

True Happiness Is Now Yours. If you sincerely said the prayer in Chapter One you have a new and living relationship with your Creator God, through His Son, Jesus Christ.

You can't even imagine the wonderful life that God has prepared for you, and the best part is that it will never end and will increase in glory everyday, in this life and for Eternity.

Chapter Two of this book will provide you with the information you need to begin your new life with Jesus. Your thinking and your reason for living will totally change. You will discover that you are an entirely new person, that the old is gone and the new has come, and this is all from God.

You will also learn how to live in victory over your defeated foe, Satan. Jesus Christ lived victoriously over the devil when He lived on earth, and then totally defeated him through His death, burial, and resurrection. Jesus's victory and authority over the devil now belong to you.

True Happiness Is <u>Now</u> Yours.....

Congratulations on your decision to return to your Creator through faith in the shed blood of Jesus Christ, His Sacrifice on the Cross for you. This is the most important decision you have ever made.

Please don't forget to record the date, time, and place of your decision to receive Jesus Christ as your Savior when you called upon the Name of the Lord to be saved. This will be a meaningful keepsake and a reminder for you, and for Satan and his demons.

Your relationship with God is now restored as if you had never sinned. You now have Christ's authority over Satan, the same as Adam and Eve had before they sinned, but that does not mean that Satan will stop trying to influence your thoughts and put doubts in your mind about your decision to return to God through Jesus Christ.

No matter how much you change and grow in your relationship with Jesus, the devil will never change. He has come to kill, steal, and destroy, and some of the tactics that he uses are fear, lying, accusations, deception, oppression, and condemnation. In the Bible, he is called "the father of lies." His power over you has been broken, but he will try to convince you that it isn't. Remember, he is a liar.

However, there is Someone else Who will never change, and that is God, His Word and His Son, Jesus, Who is the Living Word. You have no reason to fear the devil. You are now a child of God, and greater is He, Jesus, Who lives in you, than your enemy, the devil.

The first area in which the devil will try to attack and deceive you will be in the decision that you just made to receive Christ as your Lord and Savior. The battlefield will be your mind. He will place all kinds of thoughts in your mind, attempting to cause you to doubt your new relationship with God. He's afraid of you now.

He caused Adam and Eve to doubt their relationship with God, which led to their disobedience to God, which then led to separation from God. They should have exercised the authority and dominion that God had given them and answered Satan's temptation to doubt, with God's Word alone, as Jesus Christ did when He was tempted by the devil in the wilderness. Jesus is your example, not Adam and Eve.

We have already discussed Adam and Eve's temptation, but now let's examine the details of the temptation of Jesus Christ by the devil:

Jesus, full of the Holy Spirit, returned from the Jordan and was led by the Spirit in the desert, where for forty days He was tempted by the devil. He ate nothing during those days, and at the end of them He was hungry.

The devil said to Him, "If you are the Son of God, tell this stone to become bread."

Jesus answered, "It is written: 'Man does not live on bread alone, but by every Word that comes from the mouth of God.'"

The devil led Him up to a high place and showed Him in an instant all the kingdoms of the world. And he said to Him, "I will give you all their authority and splendor, for it has been given to me, and I can give it to anyone I want to. So if You worship me, it will all be Yours."

Jesus answered, "It is written: 'Worship the Lord your God and serve Him only.'"

The devil led Him to Jerusalem and had Him stand on the highest point of the temple. "If you are the Son of God," he said, "throw Yourself down from here. For it is written: '"He will command His angels concerning You to guard You carefully; they will lift You up in their hands, so that You will not strike Your foot against a stone.'"

Jesus replied, "It is written: 'Don't put the Lord your God to the test.'"

When the devil had finished all this tempting, he left Him until an opportune time. Jesus returned to Galilee in the power of the Spirit, and news about Him spread through the whole country-side. He taught in their synagogues, and everyone praised Him.

The devil even attempted to cause Jesus Christ to doubt His relationship with God. He said, **"If You are the Son of God"?** Jesus answered with the Word of God, by saying **"It is written"**.

Jesus Christ, Who was successful in defeating Satan every time He was tempted to doubt God, His Heavenly Father, is our example of how we should respond to temptations from the devil. We also answer with God's Word anytime we have thoughts or hear things, even when we feel or see things that are contrary to God's Word.

The relationship of every true child of God must be based on faith. Unbelief and a distrust of God's Word led to disobedience and sin and the separation of man from God. Therefore, faith and trust in God's Word is the only means of restoring man to God.

The Bible says, **"Without faith it is impossible to please God. We must believe that He exists, and that He is the rewarder of those who diligently seek Him."** What is faith in God? It is believing what God says is True and that God will do what He says.

The devil is a liar and he hates the Truth. He hates God Who cannot lie, and he hates faith in God and anyone who has faith in Him. He is God's enemy and also the enemy of Truth and anyone who believes in God and lives by the Truth.

Adam and Eve did not trust God and His Word when they were tempted by Satan. Rather, they listened to, believed, and acted upon his words and the thoughts he inspired rather than upon God's Word.

In Chapter One of this book, you were presented with many Truths from God's Word, the Bible, concerning how you could return to God, your Creator, and be saved from your sins and restored to God's original plan and purpose for your life, so you could experience peace, joy, and True Happiness in this life and for Eternity.

These Truths are what your faith in God must be based upon. You cannot trust in your emotions or feelings or in your intellect. You must know that you are saved and restored to God, because you believed His Word and you did what He asked you to do, period!

Keep in mind that Satan is going to bombard your mind with doubts about your salvation and new relationship with God. Your emotions and intellect will try to make you doubt, and so will other people.

However, the Holy Spirit Who now lives in you will help remind you of God's Word, and as you believe God and His Promises, God's Spirit will bear witness with your spirit that you are now His child. As you choose to believe God's Word above what you feel or think, and above what others tell you, the God of peace will be with you.

Learning how to use the authority that God has given you is very important. You want to live victoriously as a Christian, not defeated, but you must use the spiritual weapons that God has given you. Jesus Christ has won the victory for you. Therefore, you are now able to defeat Satan every time that he tempts you to doubt God's Word.

Let's have a practice session in standing firm in your new faith in God. Below are some thoughts, feelings, or words that may come your way, along with your response from God's Word:

1. You are not really saved. You must do good works to be saved. You can't just call upon Jesus and have only faith to be saved.

It is written, **"For it is by grace you have been saved, through faith, and this not from yourselves, it is the gift of God, not by works, so that no one can boast,"** and I believe God's Word.

It is written, **"Whoever calls on the Name of the Lord shall be saved,"** and I called on the Name of the Lord, and I am now saved.

It is written, **"If you confess with your mouth the Lord Jesus, and believe in your heart that God has raised Him from the dead, you shall be saved."** I did confess Jesus as Lord with my mouth, and I do believe in my heart that God raised Him from the dead, so I'm saved.

2. You are not really God's child. You are still a child of the devil, and he still has power over your life.

It is written, **"For He has rescued us from the dominion of darkness and brought us into the kingdom of the Son He loves, in Whom we have redemption, the forgiveness of sins,"** and I believe God's Word.

It is written, **"Yet to all who received Him, to those who believed in His Name, He gave the right to become children of God."** I received Jesus as my Savior and Lord, and I believed on His Name. Therefore, I am now His child. I believe His Word.

It is written, **"How great is the love the Father has lavished on us, that we should be called children of God! And that is what we are!"** I thank God for His love and His Word, and for making me His child.

3. You are not really forgiven for your sins. You have done so much wrong that God could never forgive you.

It is written, **"Therefore, there is now no condemnation for those who are in Christ Jesus, because through Christ Jesus the law of the Spirit of life set me free from the law of sin and death."** I am now in Christ Jesus and am set free from the law of sin and death.

It is written, **"I write to you, dear children, because your sins have been forgiven on account of His Name."** Thank you, Lord, that my sins are forgiven on account of Your Name.

It is written, **"And their sins and iniquities will I remember no more."** Thank you Lord that you don't even remember my sins.

4. You can't know for sure that you are saved and have Eternal Life.

It is written, **"For God so loved the world that he gave His one and only Son, that Whoever believes in Him shall not perish but have Eternal Life."** Thank you, Lord, for giving Your Son, Jesus, in my place so that I can have Eternal Life.

It is written, **"I give them Eternal Life, and they shall never perish; no one can snatch them out of My hand."** Thank you, Jesus, that Your Words are true and thank you for your Gift of Eternal Life.

It is written, **"For the wages of sin is death; but the gift of God is Eternal Life through Jesus Christ our Lord."** I believe God's Word.

It is written, **"In hope of Eternal Life, which God, that cannot lie, promised before the world began."** I believe that God cannot lie.

It is written, **"And this is the promise that He has promised us, even Eternal Life."** Thank you for Your promise of Eternal Life.

It is written, " **And this is the testimony: God has given us Eternal Life, and this Life is in His Son. He who has the Son has Life; he who does not have the Son of God does not have Life. I write these things to you who believe in the Name of the Son of God so that you may know that you have Eternal Life.**" I have received the Son of God and therefore I have Eternal Life. Thank you, God, that You want me to know for sure that I have Eternal Life.

5. Nothing has changed in your life. You are the same person you have always been, and you can't expect anything to change now.

It is written, **"Therefore, if anyone is in Christ, he is a new creation; the old has gone, the new has come! All this is from God."** I am now in Christ Jesus and therefore, I am a new creation. I thank You, God that my old life is gone, and Your new life has come. Most of all, I thank You that my new life is a free gift from You.

It is written, **"Because by one sacrifice He has made perfect forever those who are being made holy."** I thank you, God, that you see me as perfect while you are making me holy. I believe it, Lord!

It is written, **"and have put on the new self, which is being renewed in knowledge in the image of its Creator."** Thank you, God, that You are renewing me in Your Image.

We believe that these portions of God's Word will empower and enable you to defeat the enemy of your soul when he or anyone else attempts to cause you to doubt your new relationship with God. Anytime you begin to have doubts, respond by speaking God's Word in faith, and the devil and his doubts will flee from you.

The Word of God must be the controlling factor in your life, now that you have been saved and are God's child. You cannot allow your thoughts, your feelings, what you hear or see, to control your life any longer. God's Word is Truth and Truth is now your standard.

You are saved because God's Word says you are. You are God's child now because God's Word says you are His child now. You have Eternal Life because God's Word says you have it. Your sins are forgiven because God's Word says your sins are forgiven.

Here are words that will assist you in giving thanks to God through prayer for the Truth you have just learned in Chapter Two:

Dear Heavenly Father,

Thank You so much for revealing Yourself to me and for bringing me back to You through Your Son, Jesus Christ. Thank You that I can say with confidence now, on the basis of Your Word, that I am Your child, that I am a new person and now have a whole new life, that I am now saved from the penalty and power of sin, and that you don't remember my sins anymore.

Thank You, Father, that I now possess Eternal Life, as well as an abundant and blessed life right here and now. Thank you, Lord, that You did all of this for me, and none of it depends on my good works, but rather on my faith in You and what You have promised me in Your Word, the Bible. It is all a free gift from You to me, because You love me and because You want a relationship with me.

Thank you, Jesus, for all that You have done for me. Your demonstration of love towards me is beyond my comprehension and understanding, but not beyond my faith. I believe that You loved me so much that You took my place on the Cross, and I am grateful.

I also believe that You overcame Satan through your shed blood when You died on the Cross, as well as with the Word of God when You were tempted by him in the wilderness for forty days.

Thank you, Jesus, for defeating Satan on my behalf, and for demonstrating to me how I can overcome his schemes and temptations by using the Word of God, just as You did.

Please help me live by faith in Your Word, no matter what I think, feel, or hear. Jesus Christ is my example, not Adam and Eve. I choose to follow you, Lord, wherever You take me. Reveal Yourself to me more and more, and your plan for my new life. I love You!

In Jesus's Name I pray,
Amen!

True Happiness
Is God's Will For You

Chapter Three

True Happiness Is God's Will For You! God is a good and loving God and only wants good for you. Now that you understand the basis for your faith in God, and your right to be His child, you must begin to know what God is like so that you can develop an intimate relationship with Him.

Knowing what God is like will allow you to actually get to know Him in a very personal way. Being a Christian is not about religion, but rather relationship, a close relationship with your Creator through Jesus Christ, His Son.

This chapter will help you know what God is really like, not what the world, the devil, and religion tell us He is like. As the Spirit of God reveals Him to you, your love and trust for Him will grow stronger, and you will experience His Blessings and Presence in your life each day.

Knowing God personally will then lead to you knowing His perfect will and plan and purpose for your life.

True Happiness Is God's Will For You.....

Living by the Truth will become exciting to you and bring you many blessings from God, along with True Happiness, every day of your life. You have already received the greatest blessing, the Truth that you now have a living relationship with God, your Creator, through His Son, Jesus Christ. You will never be punished for your sins, but rather will spend all Eternity in Heaven with Jesus.

You are now an entirely new creature, because of your relationship with God through the Lord Jesus Christ. You will spend the rest of your life and all Eternity discovering what this actually means to you. When He saved you, God did something for you that cannot be described with mere words and cannot be comprehended or understood all at once.

You are a babe in Christ, having just been Born Again, but you will grow everyday as you feed on God's Word. The Holy Spirit, Who now lives in you, will reveal God's Word to you. He will teach you and guide you into all Truth, and you will begin discovering and exploring everything that God has done for you.

For example, God's Word teaches that you are now God's child, and therefore you are heirs with God and joint heirs with Christ. This means that the Creator of the Universe is your Heavenly Father, and that everything He has also belongs to you.

You are no longer the person you used to be. The old is gone, the new has come, and it is all from God. You may think that you are not worthy or that you don't deserve all this, but you cannot think in the old way about yourself any longer. You must realize that you are valuable to God. Your worth is based on the price that He paid to buy you back from Satan's slave market of sin.

You are valuable to God. He created you and has a plan and purpose for your life that fits into His Big Love Plan for the entire human race. He proved that you are valuable to Him by paying such a great price to redeem you. He paid with the life and the shed blood of His one and only Son. He punished the perfect Son of God in your place. He allowed Him, Jesus, to die for you and to bear your sins, sicknesses and pains so that you could be brought back to Him.

That is love beyond our comprehension. Don't ever let the devil or anyone else look down on you as someone that is worthless or of little value. Your Creator has established your value, and that settles it forever. Whenever you begin to doubt your value or worth to God, just think of Jesus dying on a Cross in your place, being beaten for your healing, and shedding His precious Blood for your sins. God loves you with an everlasting love, and you are of Infinite value and worth to Him. You are now His child forever. That's the Truth!

God's Word, the Bible, instructs us to **"fix our eyes on Jesus, the Author and Finisher of our faith, Who for the joy set before Him, endured the Cross, scorning it's shame and sat down at the right hand of God."** Your new life with God is made possible by Jesus. He said, **"I am the Way, and the Truth, and the Life, and nobody comes to the Father except by Me."** Jesus is the only way to God.

You are now a follower of Jesus. Your entire life is all about Jesus. Your faith must be in Jesus. Jesus Christ is the express image of God. The Bible says, **"The Word became flesh and made His dwelling among us. We have seen His glory, the glory of the One and Only, Who came from the Father, full of grace and truth."** Jesus Christ is the Living Word of God. You must identify with Jesus.

Jesus came to this earth to seek and to save that which was lost, which was the entire human race, including you and I. The sinless, perfect life that Jesus lived here on earth was for us all. His victory over Satan was for us all. The beatings and punishment that He received in His body was for us all. His shed blood on the Cross was for all of us, as was His death, His burial, His descent into Hell, His Resurrection, His Glorification and His Ascension into Heaven.

Jesus Christ had no reason to come to earth, except for us. He had nothing to prove and no one to impress. He had no sins of His own to die for, and when He died on a Cross, He gave His life; it was not taken from Him. His death was a voluntary act of Divine Love.

We must identify ourselves totally with Jesus in order to understand and benefit from Who He is and what He did on our behalf. One of the greatest Truths that we can ponder is His Substitution for us.

In other words, when Jesus Christ was punished and died on that Cross, you were punished and died on that Cross. When Jesus Christ was buried, you were buried. When Jesus Christ went to Hell, you went to Hell. When Jesus Christ was raised from the dead, you were raised from the dead. When Jesus Christ ascended into Heaven, you ascended into Heaven.

Everything Jesus did was for you and me. **Jesus did not come to be ministered to, but rather to minister and to give His life as a ransom for many.** He said, **"No one takes My Life from Me. I lay it down on My own accord."** When Jesus Christ died on the Cross in our place, it was a deliberate act of love by the Father and the Son.

Jesus Christ also came to earth to show God, our Heavenly Father, the Creator of the Universe, to the world. Satan had deceived mankind as to what God was really like. His lies have portrayed God much differently than He really is, a loving Heavenly Father Who wants only good for His children.

People have been running away from God for centuries, because of deception by our enemy and because of ignorance of what God is really like and how great His Love is for us all. He demonstrated His character so clearly through His Son, Jesus, Who not only is the Way for us to return to God, but Who also shows us how we, His children, should relate to our Heavenly Father in our everyday lives.

As His children, we should no longer be afraid of God. He will never punish us, because He punished Jesus in our place. **We have not been appointed to suffer God's anger, but rather to receive salvation.** As God's children we should never run and hide from Him. We should run toward Him and draw near Him.

The picture of God, as your Heavenly Father, should not come from how your earthly father has treated you. You must form your image of your Heavenly Father from the Bible, the written Word of God, and from Jesus, the Living Word of God.

You will then be able to relate to Him as you should, and be able to receive the benefits and the inheritance of being a child of God.

Here are some precious words from the Bible:

Praise the Lord, my soul! All my being, praise His Holy Name!

Praise the Lord, my soul, and do not forget all His benefits.

He forgives all my sins and heals all my diseases.

He keeps me from the grave and blesses me with love and mercy.

He fills my life with good things, so that I stay young and strong like an eagle.

The Lord judges in favor of the oppressed and gives them their rights.

The Lord is merciful and loving, slow to become angry and full of constant love.

He does not keep on rebuking; He is not angry forever. He does not punish us as we deserve or repay us according to our sins and wrongs.

As high as the sky is above the earth, so great is His love for those who honor Him.

As far as the east is from the west, so far does He remove our sins from us.

As a father is kind to his children, so the Lord is kind to those who honor Him.

Isn't this a beautiful image of our Heavenly Father? And this is only a glimpse into the love, goodness, grace, and mercy of God. This description of God was recorded many years before Jesus Christ was born, but now Jesus Himself is our best image of God.

It is written in the Bible, **"The Son is the radiance of God's glory and the exact representation of His Being, sustaining all things by His powerful Word. After He had provided purification for sins, He sat down at the right hand of the Majesty in Heaven."**

It is also written in the Bible, **"For unto us a child is born, unto us a son is given: and His Name shall be called Wonderful, Counsellor, The mighty God, The everlasting Father, The Prince of Peace."**

Jesus Himself said, **"Anyone who has seen Me has seen the Father."** God wants us to know exactly what He is like and what He has done for us so that we can have an intimate, personal relationship with Him. Then we can be all that He created us to be, and we can enjoy our lives to the fullest, here and now and for all Eternity.

Jesus also said, **"I have called you friends, for everything that I learned from My Father I have made known to you."** You are now a friend of Jesus Christ, and He wants you to know everything that He has learned from His Heavenly Father.

The Spirit of God Who now lives in you will reveal the Father and the Son to you so that you can know Him personally and intimately as you should. As it is written: **"No eye has seen, no ear has heard, no mind has conceived what God has prepared for those who love Him -- but God has revealed it to us by His Spirit. The Spirit searches all things, even the deep things of God. We have not received the spirit of the world but the Spirit Who is from God, that we may understand what God has freely given us."**

From this portion of God's Word, we learn that we do not gain a personal knowledge of God with our natural or physical senses, but rather, by revelation from the Holy Spirit of God. God wants us to know all the good things He has prepared for us and freely given us. Yes, God wants us to know Him and possess all His blessings.

It is written, **"He who spared not His own Son, but delivered Him up for us all, how shall He not with Him also freely give us all things?"** It is also written, **"No good thing will He withhold from them that walk uprightly,"** and **"Every good and perfect gift is from above, coming down from the Father of the heavenly lights, who does not change like shifting shadows."**

So we see that God always wants only good for us. Jesus Christ was beaten, suffered, and died in our place to deliver us from sin, sickness, disease, and pain, and from all the works of the devil. God now wants us to possess and experience all the good gifts and blessings that Jesus Christ faithfully purchased for us when He redeemed us from sin and its curse with His precious shed blood.

You must be convinced that it is God's will for you to now **prosper and be in health, even as your soul prospers.** This is what the Bible clearly teaches and what Jesus Christ demonstrated to everyone, when He walked and lived here on earth. The Bible tells us, **"How God anointed Jesus of Nazareth with the Holy Spirit and power, and how He went around doing good and healing all who were under the power of the devil, because God was with Him."**

Jesus healed the sick, made the blind to see, the deaf to hear, and the dumb to speak. He cast out evil spirits, raised the dead, healed the lepers, and made the lame to walk. He healed everyone who came to him in faith, no matter how serious their sickness or disease. He forgave the sins of everyone that put their trust in Him. **Jesus Christ came into this world to save sinners, and He was manifested to destroy the works of the devil.**

Jesus Christ is alive, and **is the same yesterday, today and forever.** The miracles that He performed 2,000 years ago, He still does today. Jesus was always compassionate and responsive to the needs of all with whom He met. He even supernaturally provided food for thousands when it was needed. He loved and cared for people like no one ever has or ever will. That's just the way Jesus is!

It is so important that we, as God's children, know what to expect from our Heavenly Father. His will for us is always good. It is written, **"Do not conform any longer to the pattern of this world, but be transformed by the renewing of your mind. Then you will be able to test and approve what God's will is--His good, pleasing and perfect will."** God's will is described as good, pleasing, and perfect.

Don't allow the devil or anyone else to tell you differently than what's in God's Word. Your mind will be renewed as you **fix your eyes on Jesus** Who always did only good for everyone who trusted in Him. Jesus always did the will of His Father in Heaven.

So now you know that God's will is that you be blessed, truly happy, in good heath, prosperous in every way, forgiven, and free from all the works of the devil. The reason you know is because God's Word says so, and Jesus demonstrated the will of God on earth.

Now is a good time to recap the things you have learned in Chapter Three through the following prayer of thanksgiving to God:

Dear Heavenly Father,

Thank You so much for being Who You are, and how You are, and that I can count on You to never change or ever lie. I am so thankful that True Happiness Is Your Will For Me, and that You always want only good for me, because that's just how You are. You are wonderful!

Thank You, Lord, for the Holy Spirit, Who is guiding me into all Truth and Who is revealing Jesus to me, along with all that You have prepared for me. Thank You, God, that You want me to know all about You and that you don't keep any secrets from me.

Thank You, Jesus, that You consider me to be a friend of Yours and therefore You share everything with me, so that I can know You intimately and personally, and so we can have a close relationship.

I know that I am just a babe in Christ, but I expect to grow up to be strong in the Lord as I keep my eyes fixed on Jesus. I am excited about discovering all the good things You have in store for me as I live out my new life as a Christian each day.

Thank You, Lord, that You are revealing to me how valuable I am to You. I will never let anyone tell me any differently. I am a child of God and have inherited all that is Yours. All my needs are met by You. I have an abundance, I am prosperous and healthy, and my soul is also prospering. All of this is because of Jesus and my identification with Him. Your love is beyond anything I have ever dreamed.

Thank You, Lord Jesus, that everything You came to earth to accomplish was for me and others like me. You didn't come to be ministered to, but to minister and give Yourself for me. Thanks for showing me the Father as You healed, saved, and delivered people. Thank You that I can know that You will do the same for me. I Love You!

In Jesus' Name I pray,
Amen!

True Happiness
Is Jesus In You

Chapter Four

True Happiness Is Jesus In You! The Lord Jesus Christ Who now lives in you is Everything and Everyone that you will ever need to be Truly Happy.

You have come to trust Jesus as your Savior and Lord. Now you will learn how to trust Him in all areas of your life.

Discovering Jesus in His Fullness takes a lifetime, but here in Chapter Four, you will discover many of the fundamental attributes of Jesus Christ and thereby discover your completeness in Him.

You will discover that all the fullness of the Godhead dwells bodily in Jesus and that in Him, you are complete. In other words you lack nothing; everything you will ever need is found in Christ Who lives in you.

This is an awesome Truth from God's Word. Imagine that Everything and Everyone you will ever need is living inside of you every day.

True Happiness Is Jesus In You.....

Jesus Christ now lives in you and you live in Him. The Bible says,
**"For in Him dwells all the fullness of the Godhead bodily, and
you are complete in Him."** In other words, you lack nothing. You
are now everything that God originally created you to be.

This completeness is in Jesus, and because you are in Him and He is
in you, you lack nothing. Every need you have is now met through
Christ, and then some. Christ in you is the hope of glory.

Read and meditate upon the following verses of Scripture from the
Bible, and they will help you understand how blessed you are:

The Lord is my Shepherd, I shall not be in want.

**He makes me lie down in green pastures, He leads me beside
quiet waters, He restores my soul.**

He guides me in paths of righteousness for His Name's sake.

**Even though I walk through the valley of the shadow of death, I
will fear no evil, for You are with me; Your rod and Your staff,
they comfort me.**

**You prepare a table before me in the presence of my enemies.
You anoint my head with oil; my cup overflows.**

**Surely goodness and love will follow me all the days of my life,
and I will dwell in the house of the LORD forever.**

Jesus is revealed here as the Shepherd and you are one of His sheep.
In previous chapters, we referred to you as God's child, and that you
are. However, in this chapter, we will also discuss your relationship
with Jesus Christ in other ways.

Read this portion of God's Word over and over and allow the Holy
Spirit to make this real to you. God wants to touch your innermost
being through His Word. He wants to make Himself real to you so
that He can love you and bless you more than you can imagine.

**For the Word of God is living and active. Sharper than any double-
edged sword, it penetrates even to dividing soul and spirit, joints**

and marrow; it judges the thoughts and attitudes of the heart. Nothing in all creation is hidden from God's sight. As you ponder the Word of God and His Goodness and Love revealed therein, the Spirit of God will touch you deeply, change you, and enlarge your heart and soul, enabling you to experience Christ's love even more.

Jesus is your Shepherd. He will guide you and provide for you, and comfort and bless you. You will not want. He is the Good Shepherd that leads you along the path of life and keeps you from all harm. You have no reason to fear or worry. Your Shepherd meets all your needs and protects you and blesses you with peace and joy.

Trust in the Lord with all your heart. Lean not on your own under-standing. Acknowledge Him in all your ways, and He will direct your paths. Don't trust in yourself! **There is a way that seems right unto man, but the end thereof is the way of death.** Follow Jesus. **He is the Way, the Truth and the Life.** He will never lead you astray.

Jesus will never leave you, nor ever forsake you. No one can pluck you from the Father's Hand. Neither death nor life, nei-ther angels nor demons, neither the present nor the future, nor any powers, neither height nor depth, nor anything else in all creation, will be able to separate us from the love of God that is in Christ Jesus our Lord.

You are secure in Jesus. Read and meditate upon the following por-tion of God's Word from the Bible:

He who dwells in the shelter of the Most High will rest in the shadow of the Almighty. I will say of the LORD, "He is my ref-uge and my fortress, my God, in whom I trust."

Surely He will save you from the fowler's snare and from the deadly pestilence. He will cover you with his feathers, and under His wings you will find refuge; His faithfulness will be your shield and ram-part.

You will not fear the terror of night, nor the arrow that flies by day, nor the pestilence that stalks in the darkness, nor the plague

that destroys at midday.

A thousand may fall at your side, ten thousand at your right hand, but it will not come near you. You will only observe with your eyes and see the punishment of the wicked.

If you make the Most High your dwelling-- even the LORD, Who is my refuge-- then no harm will befall you, no disaster will come near your tent. For He will command His angels concerning you to guard you in all your ways; they will lift you up in their hands, so that you will not strike your foot against a stone.

You will tread upon the lion and the cobra; you will trample the great lion and the serpent. "Because he loves me," says the LORD, "I will rescue him; I will protect him, for he acknowledges My Name.

He will call upon Me, and I will answer him; I will be with him in trouble, I will deliver him and honor him. With long life will I satisfy him and show him My Salvation."

This is the precious revelation of your relationship with your Creator, through His Son, Jesus Christ. God cares so much for you. Read these words over and over and think about what they say, and believe them as if they were written personally to you from God. The Bible is God's love letter to all who believe in Him.

No one has ever loved you like Jesus. For this reason I kneel before the Father, from whom His whole family in heaven and on earth derives its name.

I pray that out of His glorious riches He may strengthen you with power through his Spirit in your inner being, so that Christ may dwell in your heart through faith. And I pray that you, being rooted and established in love, may have power, together with all the saints, to grasp how wide and long and high and deep is the love of Christ, and to know this love that surpasses knowledge--that you may be filled to the measure of all the fullness of God.

Now to Him Who is able to do immeasurably more than all we ask or imagine, according to His power that is at work within us, to Him be glory in the church and in Christ Jesus throughout all generations, for ever and ever! Amen.

You can never exhaust the Love of God, nor His riches, nor His mercy, nor His goodness, nor His grace, nor His forgiveness, nor His power, nor His peace, which are beyond your understanding. All that God has is yours, and His resources are endless.

Everything that God has and Everything that God is are wrapped up in Jesus Who lives in you, and you in Him. **Jesus Christ is the same yesterday, today and forever.** He is alive and will do for you what He did for those who believed when He walked the earth over two thousand years ago.

Jesus came into the world to save sinners. He came to seek and to save that which was lost. **Jesus went about doing good and healing all that were oppressed by the devil.** He came to reverse the curse placed on mankind because of sin and bring restoration and reconciliation between God and us. He came to give us Eternal Life.

Eternal Life is not only forever, but it also is a quality of life here and now. God does not want us to remain in bondage to any of the effects of sin or to any of the schemes of Satan. Jesus Christ made that very clear when He healed the sick, forgave the sinner, cast out demons, fed the hungry, and met the needs of all those who believed in Him. That's what He will do for you and me today.

On one occasion, **when Jesus came into Peter's house, He saw Peter's mother-in-law lying in bed with a fever. He touched her hand and the fever left her, and she got up and began to wait on Him.**

When evening came, many who were demon-possessed were brought to Him, and He drove out the spirits with a Word and healed all the sick.

This was to fulfill what was spoken through the prophet Isaiah: "He bore our sicknesses and carried our diseases."

Centuries before Jesus was born, it was written:

Surely He bore our sicknesses and carried our diseases, yet we considered Him plagued, smitten by God, and afflicted.

But He was pierced for our transgressions, He was crushed for our iniquities; the punishment that brought us peace was upon Him, and by His wounds we are healed.

We all, like sheep, have gone astray, each of us has turned to his own way; and the LORD has laid on Him the punishment of us all.

Years after Jesus died on the Cross, it was written in God's Word:

He Himself bore our sins in His body on the tree, so that we might die to sins and live for righteousness; by His wounds you have been healed. For you were like sheep going astray, but now you have returned to the Shepherd and Overseer of your souls.

It is so important for you to understand and believe that when Jesus Christ died in your place, He suffered and died for your sins, sicknesses, diseases, and pains so you could be forgiven and healed.

It is also written, **"Beloved, I wish above all things that you will prosper and be in health, even as your soul prospers."**

God has forgiven your sins, and He has provided for the healing of your body through the suffering, death, burial, and resurrection of Jesus Christ. It is your privilege, purchased and provided by Jesus, to live in health, free from oppression by sin and Satan, just as you have the right to be forgiven for your sins.

Jesus came that you might have life and that life more abundantly. Your Heavenly Father wants you to live a full and complete life. His will is for you to live in victory, in holiness, in divine health, in prosperity, and in His love and peace that passes all understanding.

Satan came to steal, kill, and destroy, and he wants you to remain bound in sin, addictions, immorality, sickness, pain, disease, poverty, lack, turmoil, hatred, greed, lies, and all kinds of mental, physical, and emotional agony and turmoil that will rob you of God's will for your life.

You must settle in your heart and mind that you want only what God wants for your life, and that His will is always good for you. You must desire for yourself what God desires for you, and desire it for the same reason that God desires it for you, and then cooperate with the Holy Spirit so that God can bring it all to pass in your life.

You must also settle in your heart that you are going to resist Satan and all of his schemes and desires for your life by using the Word of God to defeat Him, and to know the difference between his will for your life and God's will for your life.

It is written, **"Submit yourself to God. Resist the devil and he will flee from you. Draw near to God and He will draw near to you."**

You must want what God wants for you in every area of your life, and you must believe that God will do everything that He says He will do for you, His child. Your body and your spirit were bought with a price. Therefore, you should expect God's health in body and spirit and settle for nothing less.

It is written, **"Do you not know that your body is a temple of the Holy Spirit, Who is in you, Whom you have received from God? You are not your own; you were bought at a price. Glorify God in your body, and in your spirit, which are God's."**

When God's forgiveness and healing power are manifested in your body and spirit, God is glorified. When Jesus forgives the sinner and heals the sick, God is glorified. Satan wants to rob God of His Glory by keeping people in bondage to sin, sickness, and disease, but Satan is defeated, and God's healing power and forgiveness are still available to all who will believe and take God at His Word.

To receive healing you must know that God wants you to be healed, the same as you knew that God wanted you to be forgiven and saved. God cares about the whole person that He created. He wants to meet all your needs. Jesus never ignored anyone who believed Him and asked Him to heal them, and He never will! He always healed and forgave all who believed in Him for forgiveness and healing, and He still does today.

Let's read a few accounts of Jesus's ministry when He walked the earth, over 2,000 years ago, as they are recorded in the Bible:

While Jesus was in one of the towns, a man came along who was covered with leprosy. When he saw Jesus, he fell with his face to the ground and begged him, "Lord, if you are willing, you can make me clean." Jesus reached out His hand and touched the man. "I am willing," He said. "Be clean!" And immediately the leprosy left him.

This man questioned whether or not it was the will of God for Jesus to heal him. Jesus answered clearly, **"I am willing!"** This is the same answer Jesus will give today. It is always God's will to heal.

Jesus went to a town called Nain, and his disciples and a large crowd went along with Him. As He approached the town gate, a dead person was being carried out--the only son of his mother, and she was a widow. And a large crowd from the town was with her.

When the Lord saw her, His heart went out to her and He said, "Don't cry." Then He went up and touched the coffin, and those carrying it stood still. He said, "Young man, I say to you, get up!" The dead man sat up and began to talk, and Jesus gave him back to his mother.

Jesus is so loving and compassionate that He even raises the dead.

One day Jesus said to his disciples, "Let's go over to the other side of the lake." So they got into a boat and set out. As they sailed, he fell asleep. A squall came down on the lake, so that the boat was being swamped, and they were in great danger. The disciples went and woke Him, saying, "Master, Master, we're going to drown!" He got up and rebuked the wind and the raging waters; the storm subsided, and all was calm.

Yes, even the wind and the waters obey Jesus.

As Jesus approached Jericho, a blind man was sitting by the roadside begging. When He heard the crowd going by, he asked what was happening. They told him, "Jesus of Nazareth is passing by." He called out, "Jesus, Son of David, have mercy on me!"

Those who led the way rebuked him and told him to be quiet, but he shouted all the more, "Son of David, have mercy on me!" Jesus stopped and ordered the man to be brought to Him. When he came near, Jesus asked him, "What do you want Me to do for you?" "Lord, I want to see," he replied.

Jesus said to him, "Receive your sight; your faith has healed you." Immediately he received his sight and followed Jesus, praising God. When all the people saw it, they also praised God.

Jesus acknowledged this man's faith. He believed and was healed.

This is why we stress the importance of faith in God's Word. **Without faith, it is impossible to please God.** Remember, faith is simply trusting that God will do that which He has already promised to do. It is simply taking Him at His Word. This pleases God.

A large crowd followed and pressed around Jesus. **And a woman was there who had been subject to bleeding for twelve years. She had suffered a great deal under the care of many doctors and had spent all she had, yet instead of getting better she grew worse.**

When she heard about Jesus, she came up behind Him in the crowd and touched His cloak, because she thought, "If I just touch the hem of His garment, I will be healed." Immediately her bleeding stopped and she felt in her body that she was freed from her suffering.

At once Jesus realized that power had gone out from Him. He turned around in the crowd and asked, "Who touched My clothes?" "You see the people crowding against You," his disciples answered," and yet You can ask, "Who touched Me?" But Jesus kept looking around to see who had done it.

Then the woman, knowing what had happened to her, came and fell at His feet and, trembling with fear, told Him the whole truth. He said to her, "Daughter, your faith has healed you. Go in peace and be freed from your suffering."

Again, Jesus did what the doctors couldn't do in response to this woman's faith. You too can believe and be healed.

These are just a few of the miracles that are recorded in God's Word, but **Jesus did many other things as well. If every one of them were written down, I suppose that even the whole world would not have room for the books that would be written.**

Salvation, from God's point of view, involves the saving and deliverance of the entire human being from the effects of sin and complete restoration to God's original plan for all people.

Don't limit God. Believe God's Written Word, the Bible, and God's Living Word, Jesus Christ. Make the most of all the benefits of knowing God, and give Him all the Glory for all He has done for you. Don't allow the devil to steal from you anymore. He's a liar!

The next chapter of this book will teach you how to receive all the benefits that God has freely provided for you through Jesus. You will discover how to appropriate the promises of God, and experience all the benefits of knowing Him personally. This is a good place to close Chapter Four. Let's offer a prayer of thanksgiving to God for what you have just learned:

Dear Heavenly Father,

Thank You that all Your fullness dwells bodily in Jesus. In Him, I am complete. I now have True Happiness because I have Jesus. I never again need to want for anything or anyone. I am in Jesus, and He is in me. I have Jesus, and He has me. We are now one with You.

Thank You, Lord, that you are my Shepherd and I will not want. Thank You that You are with me always and that You will never leave me. Thank You for guiding me and for protecting me and for caring for my every need. Thank You for leading me into paths of righteousness and that I no longer need to fear or worry or doubt.

Thank You, Lord, that nothing in all creation can separate me from Your love. Thank You that I now dwell under Your shadow, that no harm can come to me, and that You satisfy me with long life.

Thank You, Lord, that sickness and disease no longer have power over me. I will resist them, as I resist the devil, and I will always draw near to You for healing as I have for forgiveness, knowing that you will draw near to me and keep me according to Your Word. Thank You that your Word is alive and active in my life.

I am so thankful to know that when I see Jesus, I see You, God, and that I can always count on You to do for me, through Jesus, what You did through Jesus for those who believed when He was on earth.

Dear Lord, I will not limit You in my life. I want to know You as You really are. I will take You at Your Word and believe what You say, no matter what I see or hear or feel or think. I know that your Word is Truth and that You will never lie or deceive me in any way. I know You love me as I have never been loved before, and I love You, too.

In Jesus Name, I pray,

Amen!

True Happiness
Is Praying With Success

Chapter Five

True Happiness Is Praying With Success! Millions of people around the world pray each day, but a very small percentage ever receive an answer.

True prayer is not some religious exercise or tradition or ritual that we perform to appease a higher power or the "gods." True prayer is direct communication with our Creator, through His Son, Jesus Christ.

Learning to pray according to God's Word is essential to your success as a Christian. This is one of the most precious privileges we have, as God's children.

Anytime, anywhere, in any circumstances, we can pray and expect our Heavenly Father to hear us, and answer our prayer according to what He has promised in His Word.

This chapter will teach you how to communicate with your Heavenly Father, and receive from Him all that you need.

True Happiness Is Praying With Success.....

True prayer is direct communication with our Creator, through His Son, Jesus Christ. The prayer you prayed at the end of Chapter One restored you to a personal relationship with God. You became His child, and He became your Heavenly Father. That was the most important prayer you will ever pray.

Prayer will continue to play a vital role in your success as a child of God. You must spend time communicating with your Heavenly Father in order to get to know Him more intimately. Communication is very important in developing your personal relationship with Him.

God loves for His children to communicate with Him, and, unlike many earthly fathers, He is never too busy to listen. Prayer can be as simple as a child talking to his father and can be about any subject matter and include praise, thanksgiving, and requests for yourself and others.

The prayers at the end of each chapter have contained mostly thanksgiving and praise. You have expressed your gratitude for Who God is and what He has done for you and for the entire human race. Praise is saying back to God what He reveals to you about Himself, and then thanking Him for being Who He is.

Praise and thanksgiving are ways to vocalize and express your thoughts about, and appreciation for, God to Him. You can also sing praises and thanksgiving to God. Praise and thanksgiving can involve your entire being: your spirit, your mind, your emotions, and your body. You can shout praises to God. You can dance before the Lord. You can praise Him with musical instruments. You can raise your hands and praise Him, or you can quietly praise and thank Him.

Praise and thanksgiving come from your heart and overflow to the Lord to express your love and gratitude for Him. There is no one certain way to praise God, and there are no certain words. Praise and thanksgiving are as diverse as His children, and He loves to hear and watch you express your love and gratitude to Him.

The Bible says, **"Through Jesus, therefore, let us continually offer to God a sacrifice of praise--the fruit of lips that confess His Name."**

The Bible says, **"But you are a chosen people, a royal priesthood, a holy nation, a people belonging to God, that you may declare the praises of Him Who called you out of darkness into His wonderful light."**

The Bible also says, **"In every thing give thanks: for this is the will of God in Christ Jesus concerning you."**

You already have so much to praise and thank God for. Make your attitude one of praise and thanksgiving. Have an attitude of gratitude. You will not only give God the glory that He deserves, but you will find joy and happiness flooding your own mind and spirit. God will do special things in your life as you praise and thank Him.

True prayer is also the means of receiving from God. We have already discussed so many of the blessings that He has promised to His children. However, just like the forgiveness of sin, all His blessings must be appropriated or received by believing prayer.

For example, Jesus Christ died to pay for every person's sin, but every person isn't saved. Why? Because they don't call on the Name of the Lord in faith, as you did, asking God to save them. Although Eternal Life is a free gift, already paid for by God, everyone must receive it by faith, but not all do.

In the same way, although Jesus suffered and bore the sickness, disease, and pain of all humankind in His Body, many are not healed because they don't call upon Jesus the Healer in faith to deliver them.

We have already discussed how God, our Heavenly Father, wants to bless us, forgive us, heal us, provide for us, meet all of our needs, and guide and direct our lives, but this doesn't happen automatically. This is where asking in prayer comes into the picture. Believing prayer is how we receive the blessings that God has promised us.

The Bible says, **"This is the confidence we have in approaching God: that if we ask anything according to His will, He hears us. And if we know that He hears us--whatever we ask--we know that we have what we asked of Him."** Asking according to God's will is simply asking according to His Word, or more accurately, according to His promises.

When we ask according to the will of God, which is the Word of God, we can be assured that God will answer according to His Word. This is why we know that our prayers will be answered and that we will receive what we asked for. God loves to answer the prayers of His children.

Jesus said, **"Ask and it will be given to you; seek and you will find; knock and the door will be opened to you. For everyone who asks receives; he who seeks finds; and to him who knocks, the door will be opened. Which of you, if his son asks for bread, will give him a stone? Or if he asks for a fish, will give him a snake? If you, then, though you are evil, know how to give good gifts to your children, how much more will your Father in Heaven give good gifts to those who ask Him!"**

You can and must approach your Heavenly Father with confidence as His child. He loves you and wants only what is good for you. Remember that He sent His Son, Jesus, to die in your place, so that He could have this relationship with you. It's also important to know that God has everything that you need, unlimited resources of every kind. Nothing is too difficult for the Lord. Trust Him and draw near to Him in prayer.

On one occasion, years ago, followers of Jesus Christ asked Him to teach them how to pray. He responded: **"Your Father knows what things you have need of, before you ask Him. Therefore pray in this manner: Our Father in Heaven, hallowed be Your Name. Your Kingdom come. Your will be done in earth, as it is in Heaven. Give us this day our daily bread. And forgive us our sins, as we forgive those who sin against us. And lead us not into temptation, but deliver us from evil. Yours is the Kingdom, and the Power, and the Glory, forever. Amen."**

We learn from Jesus that God knows what we need, even before we ask Him, and that we address Him as our Father in Heaven. We are to hallow, reverence, and honor God's Name. Although God is our Father and Friend and loves us deeply, we still must show Him the honor, reverence, and respect He deserves.

We are also taught by Jesus to pray for His Kingdom and His will to come and be done on earth, just as it is in Heaven. His Kingdom is His rule and His reign and His Lordship over our lives. In other words, we pray for our Heavenly Father's rule and reign and Lordship to exist in our lives on earth, just as it is in Heaven. We pray that whatever would be happening in Heaven for us would be ours now on this earth.

This is an awesome Truth that helps us know how to pray according to God's will, His good, pleasing and perfect will. Not only do we pray for God to rule and reign in every situation here on earth, just as He does now in Heaven, but we also pray for His will to be done on earth, as it is done right now in Heaven.

For example, if you are sad or discouraged today, you would know to pray to your Heavenly Father for joy and encouragement and know this is His will for you, because this is what it would be like for you in Heaven. Sadness and discouragement don't exist in Heaven.

Also, if you are sick or in pain, you would know it is God's will for you to be well and free from pain here and now, since there is no sickness or pain in Heaven. Therefore, you can pray in confidence that God will heal you of sickness and pain.

Jesus teaches us to expect our needs to be met every day and to pray that way, believing that God will meet our needs according to His riches in glory by Christ Jesus. No matter what we need, we can pray and expect God to supply for us each and every day. Remember, **the Lord is our Shepherd and we shall not be in want.**

We are taught by Jesus that when we sin, we should pray for forgiveness, knowing that **God is faithful and just to forgive our sins and to cleanse us from all unrighteousness.** Even though we are redeemed and are now God's children, we still sin at times.

We are also taught that we should pray for, and forgive, others when they sin against us. We do so, because God has forgiven us for our sins against Him.

Jesus teaches us to pray for deliverance from evil and not be led into temptation. We are all tempted to sin. Satan is the tempter, and we are also often tempted to sin by the desires in our own heart, but temptation is not sin. We must resist sin when we are tempted, and we can pray for deliverance from evil.

Jesus told His followers, **"Watch and pray so that you will not fall into temptation. The spirit is willing, but the body is weak."**

It is also written about Jesus, **"For we do not have a high priest who is unable to sympathize with our weaknesses, but we have One Who has been tempted in every way, just as we are--yet was without sin. Let us then approach the throne of grace with confidence, so that we may receive mercy and find grace to help us in our time of need."**

Therefore, when we are tempted to sin, we identify with Jesus Christ Who is our victory over temptation and the tempter, and we approach the throne of grace with confidence, knowing that our Heavenly Father is waiting to grant us grace and mercy in our time of need.

Jesus ends His teaching on prayer with the Truth that we are trusting in our Heavenly Father's kingdom and power and glory forever. God's rule and reign and power and glory are available forever to answer our prayers. God has made the resources of Heaven available to meet our needs here on earth when we pray in faith, believing that God will do what He has promised to do for His children.

Jesus said, **"Therefore I tell you, whatever you ask for in prayer, believe that you have received it, and it will be yours."** This is very important to understand and practice. When you pray, believe that you receive what you are asking for right then. Don't wait until you see what you asked for but rather, receive your answer by faith, knowing that God has answered, and then you will see it.

Seeing is not believing, but rather believing is seeing! Jesus once told a follower named Thomas, **"You believe because you see, but blessed are those who have not seen and yet believe."** Remember, **"Now faith is being sure of what we hope for and certain of what we do not see."** Because we have confidence in our Heavenly Father's Word, we don't have to see something to believe it. This is the faith that pleases God. **"Without faith it is impossible to please God!"**

Remember that our relationship with God is based on us believing in the integrity and truthfulness of His Word. God says something or reveals something to us in His Word, the Bible, and we believe it and act upon it, regardless of what our circumstances are or what we feel, see, or think. We take God at His Word, expecting what He has promised to come to pass, especially when we pray.

The following are more words from Jesus concerning prayer:

"I tell you the truth, whatever you bind on earth will be bound in Heaven, and whatever you loose on earth will be loosed in Heaven. Again, I tell you that if two of you on earth agree about anything you ask for, it will be done for you by My Father in Heaven. For where two or three come together in My Name, there am I with them."

"I tell you the truth, anyone who has faith in Me will do what I have been doing. He will do even greater things than these, because I am going to the Father. And I will do whatever you ask in My Name, so that the Son may bring glory to the Father. You may ask Me for anything, and I will do it."

"If you abide in Me, and My Words abide in you, you can ask what you will, and it shall be done for you."

"You did not choose Me, but I chose you and appointed you to go and bear fruit--fruit that will last. Then the Father will give you whatever you ask in My Name."

"In that day you will no longer ask Me anything. I tell you the truth, My Father will give you whatever you ask in My Name. Until now you have not asked for anything in My Name. Ask and you will receive, and your joy will be complete."

We have a relationship with our Heavenly Father because of Jesus, and God answers our prayers because of Jesus. Jesus Christ is everything to us. Without Him we are nothing. This is why we approach our Heavenly Father in prayer in the Name of Jesus Christ. When we ask in the Name of Jesus, it is as if Jesus is asking the Father for us.

As you can see from the Words of Jesus above, we can approach our Heavenly Father in absolute confidence in Jesus's Name, and God will answer our prayers. When you ask in Jesus's Name, expect to receive what you ask for and more. Remember Who you are asking to help you, the Creator of the entire Universe Who created everything that you see out of nothing. He spoke, and it was!

It is written, **"Now to Him who is able to do immeasurably more than all we ask or imagine, according to His power that is at work within us."**

You no longer have to worry or be anxious about anything. It is written, **"Do not be anxious about anything, but in everything, by prayer and petition, with thanksgiving, present your requests to God. And the peace of God, which transcends all understanding, will guard your hearts and your minds in Christ Jesus."** Anytime you lack the peace of God, pray and cast all your cares upon the Lord, thanking Him as you make your requests, and His peace will be yours.

There will be times in your Christian life when you don't know what to do and you need wisdom from God. It is written, **"If any of you lacks wisdom, he should ask God, Who gives generously to all without finding fault, and it will be given to him. But when he asks, he must believe and not doubt, because he who doubts is like a wave of the sea, blown and tossed by the wind. That person should not think he will receive anything from the Lord; he is a double-minded person, unstable in all he does."** You can always ask God for wisdom, but you must expect Him to answer with the wisdom you need.

Prayer is your lifeline to God. The Bible says, **"Devote yourselves to prayer, being watchful and thankful." "For the eyes of the Lord are on the righteous and His ears are attentive to their prayer."** Develop a practice of praying daily, even several times a day. Find a quiet place where you can spend time with the Lord each day.

The following verses from God's Word speak of Jesus's time in prayer:

After Jesus had dismissed the crowd, He went up on a mountainside by Himself to pray. When evening came, He was there alone.

And in the morning, rising up a great while before day, Jesus went out, and departed into a solitary place, and there prayed.

And it came to pass in those days, that Jesus went out into a mountain to pray, and continued all night in prayer to God.

Jesus often withdrew to lonely places and prayed.

Jesus Christ made a priority of being alone with God to pray, and each of us must do the same to maintain our relationship with Him.

Let's give thanks to God right now in prayer:

Dear Heavenly Father,

I want to praise and thank You for Who You are. You are so wonderful and awesome. I marvel at Your Goodness and Glory. I am so grateful to You for allowing me to draw near You in prayer in the Name of Jesus Christ. I give praise to You for revealing Your love to me, Your child.

Thanks for inviting me in Your Word to come boldly to Your throne of grace, so that I can find mercy in my time of need. Thank You, Lord, for being so willing to hear and answer my prayers. Thank You that I am able to approach You with confidence when I come in the Name of Jesus.

I thank You, Lord, that You love to give good gifts to your children, and that You know what I need even before I ask. Thank You for making Your Will known to me in Your Word so that I can always pray according to Your Will, and therefore always expect You to answer me.

I am so thankful that it is Your Will to be unto me here on earth as it is in Heaven. I ask right now, Heavenly Father, for Your Kingdom to come and rule and reign in my life today. I thank You for forgiving me for my sins, and I choose to forgive others when they sin against me.

I ask that You provide for all my needs today according to Your riches in glory by Christ Jesus. I ask to live in divine health and prosperity according to Your Word, even as my soul is prospering. I thank You that You have provided so abundantly for me, and that You are more than enough for me, and that I don't have to worry about anything.

Thank You for your peace that surpasses all understanding and that guards my heart and mind in Christ Jesus today. I thank You that sin, sickness, and lack have no power over me, and that I am more than a conqueror today through Jesus Christ, my Lord, Savior, and Healer.

I ask You now to give me all the wisdom that I need today to live a life of faith and love for Your Glory and Honor. Thank you for the Holy Spirit Who will guide me into all Truth today. Teach me how to live in a way that is pleasing to You so that I will always be what You want me to be, and that I will always do Your Will. Thanks for hearing my prayers.

In Jesus's Name I Pray,

Amen!

True Happiness
Is Life In The Spirit

Chapter Six

True Happiness Is Life In The Spirit! The Holy Spirit has already greatly impacted your life when you received Jesus Christ as your personal Savior and Lord!

You were enlightened by the Spirit of God, and then you were born again by the Holy Spirit. He now lives in you and wants to guide and direct every aspect of your life.

You are able to soar high above your natural instincts and understanding of life because the Holy Spirit now lives in you. You have been quickened and made alive in Christ, and your possibilities are endless.

The Holy Spirit can now lead and guide you in every area of your life in ways that you never dreamed. God's Spirit has borne witness with your spirit that you are His child, and now you can be led by His Spirit in everything you do as you cooperate with Him and follow His lead.

True Happiness Is Life In The Spirit.....

Jesus Christ, knowing that He would soon lay down His Life for all mankind and return to His Father in Heaven, said this to those who had been with Him and believed in Him:

"I will ask the Father, and He will give you another Counselor to be with you forever -- the Spirit of Truth. The world cannot accept Him, because it neither sees Him nor knows Him. But you know Him, for He lives with you and will be in you. I will not leave you as orphans.

All this I have spoken while still with you. But the Counselor, the Holy Spirit, Whom the Father will send in My Name, will teach you all things and will remind you of everything I have said to you. Peace I leave with you; My peace I give you. I do not give to you as the world gives. Do not let your hearts be troubled and do not be afraid.

When the Counselor comes, Whom I will send to you from the Father, the Spirit of Truth Who goes out from the Father, He will testify about Me. And you also must testify, for you have been with Me from the beginning. All this I have told you so that you will not go astray.

I tell you the Truth: It is for your good that I am going away. Unless I go away, the Counselor will not come to you; but if I go, I will send Him to you. When He, the Spirit of Truth, comes, He will guide you into all Truth. He will not speak on His own; He will speak only what He hears, and He will tell you what is yet to come.

He will bring glory to Me by taking from what is Mine and making it known to you. All that belongs to the Father is Mine. That is why I said the Spirit will take from what is Mine and make it known to you."

Jesus Christ was present in His earthly body with His disciples on a daily basis for over three years. They learned first hand from Him, and He met all their needs. Therefore, He wanted to comfort, encourage, and assure them that as He returned to His Father in Heaven; God would still be with them, even as He was.

The Bible, God's Word, teaches us that there is One True God, manifested in Three Persons, the Father, the Son, and the Holy Spirit. It is important that we recognize each Person of the Godhead and develop a proper relationship with each as the Word teaches us.

Your first encounter with the Holy Spirit was when He began showing you your need to have a relationship with your Creator. He opened your eyes to spiritual things, quickening you while you were still dead in your sins. He revealed Jesus Christ to you as Savior, the only way to return to God.

You were Born Again, or Born of the Spirit, when you prayed to receive Jesus as your Lord and Savior. You inherited a Divine or spiritual nature from God, and could begin relating to Him. You are now alive to spiritual Truth and to an entirely new realm of life.

This new unseen Kingdom is spiritual and Heavenly, not natural and earthly, and is only revealed by the Holy Spirit to those who are born of the Spirit of God. On one occasion, when Jesus was speaking to a very religious man, He said,

"I tell you the truth, no one can see the kingdom of God unless he is born again." "How can a man be born when he is old?" The man asked. "Surely he cannot enter a second time into his mother's womb to be born!"

Jesus answered, "I tell you the truth, no one can enter the kingdom of God unless he is born of water and the Spirit. Flesh gives birth to flesh, but the Spirit gives birth to spirit. You should not be surprised at My saying, 'You must be born again.'

The wind blows wherever it pleases. You hear its sound, but you cannot tell where it comes from or where it is going. So it is with everyone born of the Spirit."

Even today, the world is full of religious people who don't understand spiritual Truth. They cannot perceive or enter the Kingdom of God. All their religious acts, traditions, and good works are futile. They must be born of the Spirit of God by receiving Jesus Christ as their personal Savior and Lord.

Always remember what Jesus said about Himself:

"I am the Way, the Truth, and the Life. No one comes to the Father, except by Me." Jesus Christ is the only way to God!

Religious people will also have difficulty understanding you and your new life and lifestyle, and you should not expect anything different. The Bible says:

The man without the Spirit does not accept the things that come from the Spirit of God, for they are foolishness to him, and he cannot understand them, because they are spiritually discerned. The spiritual man makes judgments about all things, but he himself is not subject to any man's judgment: "For who has known the mind of the Lord that he may instruct him?" But we have the mind of Christ.

Therefore, don't expect anyone, who has not been born of the Spirit of God by receiving Jesus Christ into their life as their personal Savior and Lord, to think the way you do or have the same priorities, or act the same way. Your entire way of life and thinking will probably seem foolish to them.

Also, do not submit yourself to their way of thinking, nor their lifestyle, nor their judgment of things. You now have the mind of Christ, and the Holy Spirit will help you and teach you everything you need to know to live according to the precepts of God's Kingdom.

Just as Jesus said, **"the Holy Spirit will guide you into all Truth"**. It is also written, **"No one knows the thoughts of God, except the Spirit of God."** And **"We have not received the spirit of the world but the Spirit Who is from God, that we may understand what God has freely given us."**

Believers are instructed in God's Word to rely on the Holy Spirit to teach them the Truth, not on people. **"I am writing these things to you about those who are trying to lead you astray. As for you, the Anointing you received from Him remains in you, and you do not need anyone to teach you. But as His Anointing teaches you about all things and as that Anointing is real, not counterfeit-- just as It has taught you, remain in Him."**

The Holy Spirit will always teach you the Truth and how to discern between the Truth and the lies of our enemy, Satan. You must rely on the Spirit of God and not on your own understanding or that of others who don't have the Spirit of God.

The Holy Spirit directed the writing of God's Word, the Bible, and He knows the thoughts of God. He will always direct our minds to the Truth as we acknowledge Him and trust Him completely with the direction and guidance of every aspect of our lives, in the same way that we trusted Jesus Christ with our Eternal Destiny.

We must make a daily effort to develop our relationship with the Holy Spirit, not in an intellectual, emotional, or physical sense, but rather by our spirit communicating with God's Spirit as we read, study, and meditate upon God's Word, the Bible. His Word must be a vital and integral part of our relationship with the Holy Spirit.

Remember that your enemy, Satan, is the deceiver, and he often operates as a counterfeiter. He makes his lies look like the Truth, and the only way to recognize the lies is to know the Truth. When we know God's Word, the Truth that the Holy Spirit has inspired, we can then discern lies from the devil as we compare them with the Truth.

Therefore, the Word of God is important in knowing when God is speaking to us by His Spirit. The Holy Spirit takes from what is Christ's and makes it known to us, and all that the Father has belongs to Jesus. So when the Holy Spirit communicates with our spirits, He will be speaking the mind of God, which aligns perfectly with His Word, the Bible. His written Word and His spoken Word are One.

If we think that the Holy Spirit is guiding us in something that is contrary to the written Word in any way, we know it is not God. It may be the devil trying to mislead us, or our natural intellect, our feelings, or just our natural desires wanting their way.

It is written, **"For the Word of God is living and active. Sharper than any double-edged sword, It penetrates even to dividing soul and spirit, joints and marrow; It judges the thoughts and attitudes of the heart."**

The Word of God is our safeguard in every situation. **It is a lamp unto our feet and a light unto our path.** God's Word will always reveal and confirm His Mind to us, and His good, pleasing and perfect will for our lives. His Word can separate the spiritual from the natural in our hearts, minds, emotions, and desires.

However, to receive God's direction and the leading of the Holy Spirit in our lives each day, we must completely surrender our will to His. We must want that which God wants for our lives. We must desire for ourselves that which God desires for us, and we must desire it for the same reason that God desires it for us. The Holy Spirit will then be able to communicate to us and carry out within us God's good, perfect, and pleasing will for us.

Nothing is more exciting and fulfilling than living the life that God has prepared for us. Living in perfect harmony with your Creator and Redeemer is the most peaceful and joyful experience that you can have, and this is God's desire for you. As you follow the leading of the Holy Spirit, moment by moment, you will sense God's presence and peace in your life, as well as His Fatherhood.

It is written, **"Those who live according to the sinful nature have their minds set on what that nature desires; but those who live in accordance with the Spirit have their minds set on what the Spirit desires. The mind of sinful man is death, but the mind controlled by the Spirit is life and peace."** And **"Those who are led by the Spirit of God are sons of God."**

We must set our minds on what the Spirit desires and allow the Holy Spirit to dominate and control our minds. Then we will be able to be led by the Holy Spirit in everything. We cannot dictate to God what His will for our lives should be. We must get rid of our preconceived plans and ideas and surrender our will to His.

Next, we must be ready to obey. God will not give us direction and light unless we mean to follow it. To do so would only add to our disobedience to God. We must truly desire to know God's will for the purpose of obeying, no matter what His will is.

If we become selective in our obedience to God's revealed will, we will hinder or even forfeit our ability to hear His Voice and to sense the leading of the Holy Spirit. For our good and for God's Glory, we must be ready to obey the leading and direction of the Holy Spirit in any and every situation. By doing so, we are saying with our actions that we trust our Heavenly Father completely and without question.

In addition, we must trust the Guidance of the Holy Spirit. We must believe that He is with us and directing us. We must lean upon Him with all our heart and implicitly look up into His face and expect Him to be true to us. The Bible says it this way:

"Trust in the Lord with all your heart. Lean not on your own understanding. Acknowledge Him in all your ways, and He will direct your path." It is also written, **"Blessed is the one who trusts in the Lord and whose trust is in Him. He will be like a tree planted by the water that sends out its roots by the stream. It does not fear when heat comes; its leaves are always green. It has no worries in a year of drought and never fails to bear fruit."**

We never have to be concerned about the Holy Spirit leading us in a direction that is not good for us. He has only our best interests in mind. He knows the mind of God and knows the end from the beginning, and He never makes a mistake. Learn to trust Him completely. This trust and reliance are not instantly achieved. We learn by doing, over and over again. God understands that and is patient with us.

We may stumble from time to time in our walk with the Lord, but He will not let us fall, especially when He knows that we want to know His will and His ways, and that we want to follow Him and bring glory to His Name. God will help us learn from our mistakes so that we can discern His Voice and His leading in future situations.

We begin as babies in our spiritual lives, just as we do in our physical lives. It takes a while to learn to crawl, then stand, and then walk. In the same way, walking in the Spirit takes a while to learn and do on a regular basis.

Walking in the Spirit is how we live a life pleasing to God. As His children, we want to live in a way that brings glory to our Heavenly Father and that also reveals the life of Jesus Christ to others. This is accomplished moment by moment by walking in the Spirit.

The Bible says, **"Walk in the Spirit, and you will not gratify the desires of the sinful nature." "Be imitators of God, therefore, as dearly loved children and live a life of love, just as Christ loved us and gave Himself up for us as a fragrant offering and sacrifice to God."**

We no longer live the way we did when we were in bondage to sin and the devil. It is written, **"It is for freedom that Christ has set us free. Stand firm, then, and do not let yourselves be burdened again by a yoke of slavery."**

We were slaves to sin, but now we are free to live the way God always intended for us to live. We can now live like Jesus lived, and the Holy Spirit will help us know how to live like Him, and empower and enable us to live as Jesus lived.

The Bible says, **"Those who belong to Christ Jesus have crucified the sinful nature with its passions and desires. Since we live by the Spirit, let us keep in step with the Spirit."** We no longer live according to the desires of our sinful nature. The Holy Spirit will always reveal the life of Jesus to us as we keep in step with Him.

Walking in the Spirit and keeping in step with the Spirit are both moment-by-moment decisions that we make each day. The Holy Spirit is always trying to live the life of Jesus through us. The life of Jesus is a life of love. God is love, and there is no other word that can describe the life of Jesus Christ better than the word love.

Jesus Christ didn't come to be ministered unto, but rather to minister and to give His life as a ransom for many. In the same way, we are to live God's love life as the Holy Spirit directs and empowers us.

The entire law of God is summed up in the words of Jesus: **"Love the Lord your God with all your heart, all your soul, all your mind, and all your strength, and love your neighbor as yourself."** And **"Do unto others as you would have others do unto you."**

"The fruit of the Spirit is love, joy, peace, patience, kindness, goodness, faith, gentleness and self-control." The Holy Spirit will produce the fruit of love in your life as you yield to, and obey, Him.

"Love is patient, love is kind. It does not envy, it does not boast, it is not proud. It is not rude, it is not self-seeking, it is not easily angered, it keeps no record of wrongs. Love does not delight in evil but rejoices with the truth. It always protects, always trusts, always hopes, always perseveres. Love never fails."

The love of God has been shed abroad in our hearts by the Holy Spirit, and therefore we can now love God supremely and people as we love ourselves. In other words, we obey the Holy Spirit in everything, considering what Jesus would do in every situation, and then we do that ourselves, no matter what our flesh or emotions want.

Concerning other people, whatever you would want someone else to do for you in the same situation, that's what you should do for others. The way you treat yourself is how you should treat others.

You no longer have to put yourself first in everything because Christ has made you complete and filled the void in your life. You can now put God first in everything, and others ahead of yourselves. Read, meditate upon, and obey the following portion of God's Word:

If you have any encouragement from being united with Christ, if any comfort from His love, if any fellowship with the Spirit, if any tenderness and compassion, then make my joy complete by being like-minded, having the same love, being one in spirit and purpose.

Do nothing out of selfish ambition or vain conceit, but in humility consider others better than yourselves. Each of you should look not only to your own interests, but also to the interests of others. Your attitude should be the same as that of Christ Jesus:

Who, being in very nature God, did not consider equality with God something to be grasped, but made Himself nothing, taking the very nature of a servant, being made in human likeness. And being found in appearance as a man, He humbled Himself and became obedient to death-- even death on a cross!

Therefore God exalted Him to the highest place and gave Him the Name that is above every Name, that at the Name of Jesus every knee should bow, in heaven and on earth and under the earth, and every tongue confess that Jesus Christ is Lord, to the glory of God the Father.

Read and obey the following Words of Jesus, and you will be blessed:

"I tell you who hear Me: Love your enemies, do good to those who hate you, bless those who curse you, pray for those who mistreat you.

If someone strikes you on one cheek, turn to him the other also. If someone takes your shirt, do not stop him from taking your coat. Give to everyone who asks you, and if anyone takes what belongs to you, do not demand it back. Do to others as you would have them do to you.

"If you love those who love you, what credit is that to you? Even 'sinners' love those who love them. And if you do good to those who are good to you, what credit is that to you? Even 'sinners' do that. And if you lend to those from whom you expect repayment, what credit is that to you? Even 'sinners' lend to 'sinners,' expecting to be repaid in full.

But love your enemies, do good to them, and lend to them without expecting to get anything back. Then your reward will be great, and you will be sons of the Most High, because He is kind to the ungrateful and wicked. Be merciful, just as your Father is merciful.

"Do not judge, and you will not be judged. Do not condemn, and you will not be condemned. Forgive, and you will be forgiven. Give, and it will be given to you. A good measure, pressed down, shaken together and running over, will be poured into your lap. For with the measure you use, it will be measured to you."

The Holy Spirit will always lead us and prompt us to imitate Jesus Christ in our lives each day and to obey His teachings. Obey the Holy Spirit, and you will sense His Presence and direction in your life more and more until you develop a truly intimate relationship with your Heavenly Father, Jesus, and the Holy Spirit.

Remember that the Holy Spirit is a Divine Being, a Person that you cannot see, but Who is more real than anyone you can touch or see. He will not force Himself on you. You must be sensitive to His Presence in your life and allow Him to make Jesus known to you.

How you live as a child of God is very important. The following portion of God's Word will give you some guidance and help you to not grieve the Holy Spirit:

Do not let any unwholesome talk come out of your mouths, but only what is helpful for building others up according to their needs, that it may benefit those who listen.

And do not grieve the Holy Spirit of God, with Whom you were sealed for the day of redemption. Get rid of all bitterness, rage and anger, brawling and slander, along with every form of malice. Be kind and compassionate to one another, forgiving each other, just as in Christ God forgave you.

Be imitators of God, therefore, as dearly loved children and live a life of love, just as Christ loved us and gave Himself up for us as a fragrant offering and sacrifice to God.

But among you there must not be even a hint of sexual immorality, or of any kind of impurity, or of greed, because these are improper for God's holy people. Nor should there be obscenity, foolish talk or coarse joking, which are out of place, but rather thanksgiving.

For of this you can be sure: No immoral, impure or greedy person--such a man is an idolater--has any inheritance in the Kingdom of Christ and of God. Let no one deceive you with empty words, for because of such things God's wrath comes on those who are disobedient. Therefore do not be partners with them.

For you were once darkness, but now you are light in the Lord. Live as children of light (for the fruit of the light consists in all goodness, righteousness and truth) and find out what pleases the Lord. Have nothing to do with the fruitless deeds of darkness, but rather expose them.

In this chapter you have begun to learn Who the Holy Spirit is and how to develop an intimate relationship with Him, and thereby experience True Happiness. In the next chapter, you will learn of other aspects of the ministry of the Holy Spirit in your life. Before you pray, please read the following words of Jesus Christ:

"So I say to you: Ask and it will be given to you; seek and you will find; knock and the door will be opened to you. For everyone who asks receives; he who seeks finds; and to him who knocks, the door will be opened. "Which of you fathers, if your son asks for a fish, will give him a snake instead? Or if he asks for an egg, will give him a scorpion? If you then, though you are evil, know how to give good gifts to your children, how much more will your Father in Heaven give the Holy Spirit to those who ask Him!"

The following prayer can assist you in the growth of your relationship with the Holy Spirit:

Dear Heavenly Father,

I want to thank You for drawing me to Yourself by the Holy Spirit, and for giving me the gift of Eternal Life through my new spiritual birth. Thank You for promising to give the Holy Spirit to anyone who asks. I therefore ask right now for the Holy Spirit to come into my life and to guide, direct, fill, and control every area of my life, to reveal Jesus to me, and to show me how to live for You.

Thank You for always keeping your promise, and thank You that the Holy Spirit is now in my life making Jesus more and more real to me. Help me to be sensitive to the Holy Spirit and to not grieve Him in any way. I hereby acknowledge His Presence in my life. I trust You Holy Spirit to lead me and guide me into all Truth, and to reveal Jesus in and through my life each day.

I thank You, God, for the Spirit of Truth and that I now have the mind of Christ, and therefore can discern and judge between the Truth and a lie. I thank You, God, that I can always test a spirit by the Word of God to know whether it is You leading me, or another spirit attempting to mislead me. I want to always know Your will and do it.

Thank You, Father, that Your love has been shed abroad in my heart by the Holy Spirit, and that I can now live a life of love towards You, and other people. I know that I am complete in Jesus, and therefore I can put You first and others before me.

I choose to yield myself to the Holy Spirit and desire to see the fruit of the Spirit manifested in my life, so that You will be glorified in and through me so that others can benefit from my life.

I want my life to be used by You, Lord, and trust You to empower me and change me in whatever way is necessary to make me useful for You. I love you, God, and am so thankful that I belong to You!

In Jesus's Name I Pray,
Amen!

True Happiness
Is Partnership With God

Chapter Seven

True Happiness Is Partnership With God! Living in partnership with our Creator is the most rewarding of life's experiences. This is how we reach our full potential and highest purpose as children of God.

No experience in our lifetime can compare with the times when we are living in partnership with God. Our daily participation with God in fulfilling His plans and purposes for our lives and the lives of others that we touch, bring us the deepest joy and True Happiness.

Living life outside of relationship and partnership with God caused your life to be empty and meaningless, but when you received Jesus and were Born Again, you became a partner with God. You are ready to live supernaturally, hand in hand with Him by the power of the Holy Spirit.

The disciples went out and preached everywhere, and the Lord <u>worked with them</u> and confirmed His Word by the signs that accompanied It, and He now wants to work with you.

True Happiness Is Partnership With God.....

In the previous chapter, we discussed some aspects of the ministry of the Holy Spirit in your life, especially those pertaining to your living in personal victory over the world, the flesh, and the devil, and His moment-by-moment guidance in your life. We now want to move on to what is possibly the most important part of your Christian life: living in partnership with God by the power of the Holy Spirit.

This is how life was always meant to be between God and people: God working with people to accomplish His purposes on earth. Remember in Chapter One:

"Adam and Eve had wonderfully blessed lives as they reigned together with their Creator. God gave them dominion over all living creatures on the earth and told them to be fruitful, multiply, fill the earth, and subdue it. God basically placed them in charge of everything, even down to the naming of the animals."

We now have an even higher calling and purpose to perform as children of God. Since Jesus redeemed us by dying in our place and bought us back with His Own Precious Blood, we are not our own any longer but are set apart for the high and holy purpose of helping others come to know Jesus Christ, too.

We do this by allowing God to live His Life through us in the same way that He lived His Life through Jesus when He was here on earth. Making God known to the human race is a supernatural task that can only be accomplished by the Holy Spirit. The same Holy Spirit that worked through Jesus Christ now wants to work through us to reveal God to people everywhere.

When Jesus returned to His Father in Heaven, He commissioned His followers, which includes us today, to go into all the world and tell the Good News about Him to all people everywhere so that they could also believe, receive Him, and be saved, like us.

The Bible says, **"Everyone who calls on the Name of the Lord will be saved. How, then, can they call on the One they have not believed in? And how can they believe in the One of Whom they have not heard? And how can they hear without someone preaching to them?"**

You are vital to God's plan of making Jesus known to others. It is through partnership with you that God wants to proclaim the Good News about Jesus to others around you. Now that you have been saved and have come to know Jesus, your purpose in life is to make Jesus Christ known to others by telling them about Him.

It would not be right for you to receive all these blessings from God and then not share them with others that you come in contact with. Jesus Christ died for everyone's sins. Therefore everyone must know this Good News. You cannot allow anyone to die in sin and go to Hell forever without having the same chance to receive Jesus Christ that you had.

The greatest act of love that one human being can perform for another is to tell them the Good News about Jesus Christ, so that they also can believe in, receive, and call on the Name of the Lord to be saved. But they cannot call upon Jesus if they have not heard that He died in their place in payment for all their sins, and that He is the one and only way to return to their Creator, God.

God's primary reason for leaving you here on earth and not taking you to Heaven right now is so that you can make Jesus known to others. God used someone to bring the Gospel to you and now wants to use you to do the same for others whom He will reach with the Good News through you.

Let's study the following portion of God's Word, which will reveal much to you about God's plan to reach others through you:

Therefore, if anyone is in Christ, he is a new creation; the old has gone, the new has come! All this is from God, who reconciled us to Himself through Christ and gave us the ministry of reconciliation: that God was reconciling the world to Himself in Christ, not counting men's sins against them. And He has committed to us the message of reconciliation. We are therefore Christ's ambassadors, as though God were making His appeal through us. We implore you on Christ's behalf: Be reconciled to God. God made Him Who had no sin to be sin for us, so that in Him we might become the righteousness of God.

These words begin by reminding us that you are a new creature in Christ. Your old life is gone. You have an entirely new life, and this is all from God. He has reconciled you to Himself. God has not only brought you back to Him, but He has changed you so that you can have fellowship and live in partnership with Him.

Not only has God reconciled you to Him, but He has then given you the ministry of reconciliation, along with the rest of us believers. This is a service that you can now perform for others, for their good, on behalf of Jesus Christ and for His Glory.

You are now an ambassador for Christ, a representative of God. This is an awesome privilege and power that God has bestowed upon you. You are a messenger of hope, peace, and life to lost and dying souls wherever you go. As an ambassador for Christ, you have everything you need to accomplish the ministry of reconciliation. You can go in Jesus' Name, expecting God to work through you supernaturally in making Christ known to others. His Authority is now yours.

He has not only given you the ministry of reconciliation, but God has also committed the message of reconciliation to you: **"that God was reconciling the world to Himself in Christ, not counting men's sins against them."** This message is what you tell others so that they can also hear of the goodness of God and the gift of His Son, Jesus, on their behalf. It is only when they hear this Good News that they will know they can now be restored to their Creator.

Most people know about their sins, and they are running from God because of it. They haven't yet heard that God has reconciled them to Him through Christ and that He is no longer counting their sins against them. As people hear this wonderful news, they will want to return to God and take their rightful place as His child.

But they must hear, and God has chosen you to tell them, the Good News about Jesus Who died on the Cross in their place and suffered their punishment so that they wouldn't have to suffer. They must hear from you about the precious Blood that Jesus shed to pay for their sins, and to buy them back from the slave market of sin. They cannot believe in Someone of Whom they have not heard.

They must hear from you that, **"God was reconciling the world to Himself in Christ, not counting men's sins against them."**

They must hear from you that, **"God made Him Who had no sin to be sin for us, so that in Him we might become the righteousness of God."**

They must hear from you, **"For God so loved the world that He gave His one and only Son, that whoever believes in Him shall not perish but have eternal life. For God did not send His Son into the world to condemn the world, but to save the world through Him."**

They must hear from you, **"That the wages of sin is death, but the Gift of God is Eternal Life through Christ Jesus our Lord."**

They must hear from you, **"It is by grace you have been saved, through faith--and this not from yourselves, it is the gift of God--not by works, so that no one can boast."**

They must hear from you, **"He who has the Son has life; he who does not have the Son of God does not have life."**

They must hear from you, **"That if you confess with your mouth, "Jesus is Lord," and believe in your heart that God raised Him from the dead, you will be saved."**

They must hear from you, **"Everyone who calls on the Name of the Lord will be saved."**

They must hear from you, **"All who received Him (Jesus), to those who believed in His Name, He gave the right to become children of God--children born not of natural descent, nor of human decision or a husband's will, but born of God."**

Remember, **"Faith comes by hearing, and hearing by the Word of God."** Therefore, you must proclaim the Truth of God's Word to those you come in contact with each day. When they hear what Jesus is like and what He has done for them, they will be able to run to God and embrace His Gift of Eternal Life instead of running and hiding from Him because of their sins and the devil's deception.

God is no respecter of persons. What He has done for you, He wants to do for others through you. God's primary reason for leaving you on earth, after saving you, is to allow you to participate with Him in sharing the Good News about Jesus with others you come in contact with. **"Freely you have received, therefore freely give."**

It is written, **"Praise be to the God and Father of our Lord Jesus Christ, the Father of compassion and the God of all comfort, Who comforts us in all our troubles, so that we can comfort those in any trouble with the comfort we ourselves have received from God."**

The grace, mercy, peace, comfort, and forgiveness that you have received from God is now yours to pass on to others. This is God's plan and His purpose for your life; pass on to others all that God has given you. True Happiness will become most evident in your life when you become the instrument to bring True Happiness to others.

In the beginning, **"God blessed them, and God said unto them, Be fruitful, and multiply."** And Jesus Christ said, **"You did not choose me, but I chose you and appointed you to go and bear fruit--fruit that will last. Then the Father will give you whatever you ask in My Name."**

God's plan has always been for His children to receive His blessings and then pass them on to others. God wants to live His life through you, doing through you what He did through Jesus. As you proclaim to others the same Good News that you believe, then they can also believe in, and receive, Jesus Christ as their Lord and Savior.

Jesus Christ said, **"I tell you the truth, anyone who has faith in Me will do what I have been doing. He will do even greater things than these, because I am going to the Father. And I will do whatever you ask in My Name, so that the Son may bring glory to the Father. You may ask Me for anything in My Name, and I will do it."**

Jesus also said, **"Remain in Me, and I will remain in you. No branch can bear fruit by itself; it must remain in the vine. Neither can you bear fruit unless you remain in Me. I am the vine; you are the branches. If a man remains in Me and I in him, he will bear much fruit; apart from Me you can do nothing."**

All of the power, love, and boldness that we need come to us from the Holy Spirit, as we remain in Christ and trust the Holy Spirit to empower us and live the life of Jesus Christ through us. We cannot do the works that Jesus did in our own strength or power. **Without Him, we can do nothing.** We must remain in Him.

One of the last commands that Jesus gave His followers was:

Jesus said to them, "Go into all the world and preach the good news to every person. Whoever believes and is baptized will be saved, but whoever does not believe will be condemned.

And these signs will accompany those who believe: In My Name they will drive out demons; they will speak in new tongues; they will pick up snakes with their hands; and when they drink deadly poison, it will not hurt them at all; they will place their hands on sick people, and they will get well."

After the Lord Jesus had spoken to them, he was taken up into Heaven and He sat at the right hand of God. Then the disciples went out and preached everywhere, and the Lord worked with them and confirmed His Word by the signs that accompanied it.

It is exciting to read how Jesus commanded them to go preach to everyone everywhere and how He worked with them from Heaven to confirm His Word, with signs following as they proclaimed It. The Scriptures below help us see the role of the Holy Spirit in all of this and how essential He is to our success as Christ's ambassadors:

"Do not leave Jerusalem, but wait for the gift my Father promised, which you have heard Me speak about. For John baptized with water, but in a few days you will be baptized with the Holy Spirit. You will receive power when the Holy Spirit comes on you; and you will be My witnesses in Jerusalem, and in all Judea and Samaria, and to the ends of the earth. After He said this, He was taken up before their very eyes, and a cloud hid Him from their sight."

The first followers of Jesus Christ did exactly what He told them to do. They waited and they prayed, and God did exactly what He promised. Here's the record in God's Word of how this happened:

"When the day of Pentecost came, they were all together in one place. Suddenly a sound like the blowing of a violent wind came from Heaven and filled the whole house where they were sitting. They saw what seemed to be tongues of fire that separated and came to rest on each of them. All of them were filled with the Holy Spirit and began to speak in other tongues as the Spirit enabled them.

Now there were staying in Jerusalem God-fearing Jews from every nation under Heaven. When they heard this sound, a crowd came together in bewilderment, because each one heard them speaking in his own language.

Utterly amazed, they asked: "Are not all these men who are speaking Galileans? Then how is it that each of us hears them in his own native language? Parthians, Medes and Elamites; residents of Mesopotamia, Judea and Cappadocia, Pontus and Asia, Phrygia and Pamphylia, Egypt and the parts of Libya near Cyrene; visitors from Rome (both Jews and converts to Judaism); Cretans and Arabs--we hear them declaring the wonders of God in our own tongues!"

The Good News about Jesus was proclaimed by ordinary people empowered by the Holy Spirit to people from all over the world. Here is the account from God's Word as to what happened next as they preached and witnessed about Jesus:

"Men of Israel, listen to this: Jesus of Nazareth was a man accredited by God to you by miracles, wonders and signs, which God did among you through Him, as you yourselves know. This Man was handed over to you by God's set purpose and foreknowledge; and you, with the help of wicked men, put Him to death by nailing Him to the Cross. But God raised Him from the dead, freeing Him from the agony of death, because it was impossible for death to keep its hold on Him.

God has raised this Jesus to life, and we are all witnesses of the fact. Exalted to the right hand of God, He has received from the Father the promised Holy Spirit and has poured out what you now see and hear. "Therefore let all Israel be assured of this: God has made this Jesus, whom you crucified, both Lord and Christ."

When the people heard this, they were cut to the heart and said to Peter and the other apostles, "Brothers, what shall we do?" Peter replied, "Repent and be baptized, every one of you, in the Name of Jesus Christ for the forgiveness of your sins. And you will receive the gift of the Holy Spirit. The promise is for you and your children and for all who are far off--for all whom the Lord our God will call."

With many other words he warned them; and he pleaded with them, "Save yourselves from this corrupt generation." Those who accepted his message were baptized, and about three thousand were added to their number that day.

They devoted themselves to the apostles' teaching and to the fellowship, to the breaking of bread and to prayer. Everyone was filled with awe, and many wonders and miraculous signs were done by the apostles. All the believers were together and had everything in common. Selling their possessions and goods, they gave to anyone as he had need. Every day they continued to meet together in the temple courts. They broke bread in their homes and ate together with glad and sincere hearts, praising God and enjoying the favor of all the people. And the Lord added to the Church daily those who were being saved.

Here we read the Biblical account of the beginnings of Christianity. Thousands of people believed in Jesus Christ and were baptized and added to the Church. (You can read more about Baptism and the Church in the Appendix of this book). The lives of these people were changed forever. Signs, wonders, and miracles occurred in Jesus's Name, and everyone was filled with awe. The Holy Spirit was now doing, through the believers, that which He had done through Jesus when He was on earth, and this continued.

One day Peter and John were going up to the temple at the time of prayer--at three in the afternoon. Now a man crippled from birth was being carried to the temple gate called Beautiful, where he was put every day to beg from those going into the temple courts. When he saw Peter and John about to enter, he asked them for money. Peter looked straight at him, as did John. Then Peter said, "Look at us!" So the man gave them his attention, expecting to get something from them. Then Peter said, "Silver or gold I do not have, but what I have I give you. In the Name of Jesus Christ of Nazareth, walk."

Taking him by the right hand, he helped him up, and instantly the man's feet and ankles became strong. He jumped to his feet and began to walk. Then he went with them into the temple courts, walking and jumping, and praising God. When all the people saw him walking and praising God, they recognized him as the same man who used to sit begging at the temple gate called Beautiful, and they were filled with wonder and amazement at what had happened to him. And as the lame man which was healed held Peter and John, all the people were astonished and came running to them in the place called Solomon's Colonnade.

When Peter saw this, he said to them: "Why does this surprise you? Why do you stare at us as if by our own power or godliness we had made this man walk? God has glorified His servant Jesus. You handed Him over to be killed, and you disowned Him before Pilate, though he had decided to let him go. You disowned the Holy and Righteous One and asked that a murderer be released to you. You killed the author of life, but God raised Him from the dead. We are witnesses of this.

By faith in the Name of Jesus, this man whom you see and know was made strong. It is Jesus's Name and the faith that comes through Him that has given this complete healing to him, as you can all see. "Now, brothers, I know that you acted in ignorance, as did your leaders. But this is how God fulfilled what He had foretold through all the prophets, saying that His Christ would suffer. Repent, then, and turn to God, so that your sins may be wiped out, that times of refreshing may come from the Lord, and that He may send the Christ, Who has been appointed for you--even Jesus.

Then Peter and John were arrested by the religious leaders of that day. **But many who heard the message believed, and the number of men grew to about five thousand.** The number of believers continued to grow despite persecution and opposition.

The next day the rulers had Peter and John brought before them and began to question them: "By what power or what name did you do this?" Then Peter, filled with the Holy Spirit, said to them: "Rulers and elders of the people! If we are being called to account today for an act of kindness shown to a cripple and are asked how he was healed, then know this, you and all the people of Israel: It is by the Name of Jesus Christ of Nazareth, Whom you crucified but Whom God raised from the dead, that this man stands before you healed.

Salvation is found in no one else, for there is no other name under Heaven given to men by which we must be saved." When they saw the courage of Peter and John and realized that they were unschooled, ordinary men, they were astonished and they took note that these men had been with Jesus. But since they could see the man who had been healed standing there with them, there was nothing they could say.

The rulers and the authorities finally released the believers, commanding them not to speak in Jesus's Name any longer, but Peter and John returned to the other believers and joined them in this prayer:

"Now, Lord, consider their threats and enable your servants to speak Your Word with great boldness. Stretch out Your hand to heal and perform miraculous signs and wonders through the Name of your Holy Servant Jesus."

After they prayed, the place where they were meeting was shaken. And they were all filled with the Holy Spirit and spoke the Word of God boldly. All the believers were one in heart and mind. No one claimed that any of his possessions was his own, but they shared everything they had.

With great power the apostles continued to testify to the resurrection of the Lord Jesus, and much grace was upon them all. There were no needy persons among them. For from time to time those who owned lands or houses sold them, brought the money from the sales and put it at the apostles' feet, and it was distributed to anyone as he had need.

The same Holy Spirit that revealed God and His mighty power to the world in the days when Jesus was on earth now did the same things, in and through the lives of believers after Jesus returned to Heaven.

It is written, **"Jesus Christ is the same yesterday, today and forever."** And **"The same Spirit that raised Jesus from the dead, will also quicken your mortal bodies."** The same Holy Spirit, who now lives in you, wants to manifest the life of Jesus Christ through you today.

The boldness, love, and power of the believers in the early days of Christianity were supplied by the Holy Spirit, and are also available to you and me today so that we can also be the witnesses that God wants us to be in our generation, among our families, our friends, and all those with whom we come in contact each day.

"True Happiness Is Partnership With God." We partner with Him and He partners with us as we allow Him to work in and through us by the Holy Spirit as we go and proclaim the Good News about Jesus to others. He then works with us, confirming His Word with signs following.

As you allow God to fulfill His purposes for you in your lifetime, you will be filled with an indescribable joy that will bring you more True Happiness than you ever knew was possible. Yet this True Happiness will not even begin to compare with the Glory you will experience on that day when you arrive in Heaven with Jesus, and you see Him face to face and He says to you:

"Well done my good and faithful servant. You have been faithful with a few things; I will put you in charge of many things. Come and share your Master's Happiness!"

You may have started out reading this book just to fill a void in your life, but you have now discovered that life is so much more than you ever dreamed it could or would be, all because of Jesus. Don't let this opportunity slip away, and don't let Satan deceive you anymore.

Take hold of that for which God has taken hold of you. Make the most of all that God has now caused you to be. Live Eternal Life to It's fullest. **Draw near to God and He will draw near to you.**

After reading the appendix, you will have an opportunity to request a free copy of God's Word so that you can read and study it and then go and do what it says, but even now you must begin to act upon, and put into practice, all that you have read and learned. Read this book over and over and order more copies, free of charge, so that you can pass them on to others who are still without Jesus. Remember, **"Freely you have received, therefore freely give."**

Here's a prayer that will now help you consecrate yourself to God for a life of service in partnership with Him:

Dear Heavenly Father,

Thank You so much for giving your Son, Jesus, to die in my place so that I could return to You and become your child. I am so grateful for Your love and for Your provision for my life in every way. Thank You for taking care of me and for abundantly meeting all my needs.

But now, Lord, I understand that You didn't just save me for myself but have saved me so that You can live through me by the Holy Spirit and so that others can also have all that You have given me.

I know that being an ambassador for Christ is an awesome privilege, and I receive this calling from you today with humility, knowing that it is only by Your Power that I can fulfill this responsibility.

Therefore, I ask You now to fill me with Your Holy Spirit, imparting to me all that I need from You, to be all that You have called me to be. I open my life to You right now, Holy Spirit, and I invite You to come into my life and fill, control, and empower me so that Jesus Christ will be glorified in and through my life, as I proclaim Him to others.

Thank you, Jesus, for baptizing me with the Holy Spirit as You promised to do. I receive the Holy Spirit by faith in Your Word right now, and I believe that I am now empowered by God to serve others in Jesus's Name and that as I tell others the Good News about Jesus, lay hands on the sick, and cast out demons in Jesus's Name, You will work with me, confirming Your Word with signs following.

I believe that the fruit of the Spirit will be manifested in and through my life, as I walk in the Spirit and keep in step with the Holy Spirit. I commit myself to loving God supremely and my neighbor as myself.

Holy Spirit, use my life anyway, anytime, and anywhere you desire. Manifest Your gifts and the life of Jesus through my life, as I seek to follow Your direction and be all that God has called me to be.

In Jesus's Name,   AMEN!

Appendix

In this Appendix, a few other subjects need to be addressed to help you become a fruitful Christian and an ambassador for Christ who rightly represents Jesus.

The first subject we will address is Baptism. According to the Bible, when people are baptized, they are lowered under water for a brief moment and then raised back up above the water. This is done in obedience to Jesus's command to His followers:

Jesus said to them, "Go into all the world and preach the good news to all creation. Whoever believes and is baptized will be saved, but whoever does not believe will be condemned.

Then Jesus came to them and said, "All authority in heaven and on earth has been given to Me. Therefore go and make disciples of all nations, baptizing them in the Name of the Father and of the Son and of the Holy Spirit, and teaching them to obey everything I have commanded you. And surely I am with you always, to the very end of the age."

The act of baptism is a new Christian's way of publicly declaring and confirming his or her choice to receive Jesus Christ as Savior and Lord. This outward physical act is representative of what has already taken place inwardly and spiritually with the new believer.

The following portions of Scripture from the Bible demonstrate that it was a common practice to baptize people after they believed:

Peter replied, "Repent and be baptized, every one of you, in the Name of Jesus Christ for the forgiveness of your sins. And you will receive the Gift of the Holy Spirit. Those who accepted his message were baptized, and about 3,000 were added to their number that day.

But when they believed Philip as he preached the good news of the king-

dom of God and the Name of Jesus Christ, they were baptized, both men and women.

Then Philip began with that very passage of Scripture and told him the good news about Jesus. As they traveled along the road, they came to some water and the eunuch said, "Look, here is water. Why shouldn't I be baptized?" And Philip said, If you believe with all your heart, you may. And he answered and said, "I believe that Jesus Christ is the Son of God." And he gave orders to stop the chariot. Then both Philip and the eunuch went down into the water and Philip baptized him.

"Can anyone keep these people from being baptized with water? They have received the Holy Spirit just as we have." So he ordered that they be baptized in the name of Jesus Christ. Then they asked Peter to stay with them for a few days.

Crispus, the synagogue ruler, and his entire household believed in the Lord; and many of the Corinthians who heard him believed and were baptized.

The act of baptism is a believer's way of identifying with the substitutionary death, burial, and resurrection of the Lord Jesus Christ.

"Or don't you know that all of us who were baptized into Christ Jesus were baptized into his death? We were therefore buried with him through baptism into death in order that, just as Christ was raised from the dead through the glory of the Father, we too may live a new life."

Therefore, you will want to be obedient to Christ's command to be baptized. This is a wonderful way to declare your new life in Christ to others. Pray that God will direct you to a fellow believer, that you would like to baptize you, maybe the person who gave you this book.

It is also important for you to meet with other followers of Jesus Christ on a regular basis. Fellowship with other Christians who love Jesus and His Word can help strengthen you and them. What God has done for you in Christ can be a great encouragement to other believers, and what God has done in the lives of other believers will be an encouragement and blessing to you.

As you have read in Chapter Seven, the new believers would meet together daily for fellowship and prayer, to eat together, to listen to, and learn, God's Word, to sing praises to God, to meet one another's material and spiritual needs, and to go out and share the Good News about Jesus with others who had not yet heard it.

"Praising God, and having favor with all the people. And the Lord added to the Church daily such as should be saved."

"Peter therefore was kept in prison: but prayer was made without ceasing of the Church unto God for him."

The believers met in different places at different times. Where they assembled wasn't important, but rather that they did regularly, especially so that the believers who were stronger could help those who were weaker. Those who had been entrusted with God's resources could share with those who were in need.

Nowadays the building where believers meet is often called the Church, but the Bible teaches that the Church is a group of believers of Jesus Christ. The Church is the actual people, not the building or house in which they meet.

"The God who made the world and everything in it is the Lord of heaven and earth and does not live in temples built by hands."

Jesus said, **"For where two or three come together in My Name, there am I with them."** God's Spirit will be with you in a special way when you join together in Jesus's Name to worship God, to build each other up, and to encourage one another in your walks with the Lord.

It is also important to remember that you are the temple of the Holy Spirit. God lives and resides in you by His Spirit. He is such a loving and personal God. Be very sensitive to the Spirit of God within you, not only when you are alone, but also when you meet together with other believers. Honor God with your body.

"Do you not know that your body is a temple of the Holy Spirit, Who is in you, Whom you have received from God? You are not your own; you were bought at a price. Therefore honor God with your body."

In Chapter Seven, you read how the Holy Spirit worked through the early followers of Jesus, revealing Him to unbelievers everywhere they went. This went on daily. They fellowshipped together, meeting the needs of one another, encouraging each other, and then they went out and proclaimed the Good News about Jesus to others.

This is what your life is now all about: making Jesus known to others in both Word and deed. You are God's chosen vessel, not only to live in, but to live through. The Jesus Who lives in you is now the hope for those you come in contact with each day. You are special and God needs you to carry out His plan and will on earth.

Give yourself entirely to living for God. It won't always be easy, but it will always be worth it. You may be persecuted by others as many Christians have been, but the glory that will be revealed in you far surpasses any light and momentary troubles you may experience. Read the recorded words of one great servant of God:

"For we do not preach ourselves, but Jesus Christ as Lord, and ourselves as your servants for Jesus' sake. For God, who said, "Let light shine out of darkness," made His light shine in our hearts to give us the light of the knowledge of the glory of God in the face of Christ. But we have this treasure in jars of clay to show that this all-surpassing power is from God and not from us.

We are hard pressed on every side, but not crushed; perplexed, but not in despair; persecuted, but not abandoned; struck down, but not destroyed. We always carry around in our body the death of Jesus, so that the life of Jesus may also be revealed in our body.

It is written: "I believed; therefore I have spoken." With that same spirit of faith we also believe and therefore speak, because we know that the One who raised the Lord Jesus from the dead will also raise us with Jesus and present us with you in His presence.

All this is for your benefit, so that the grace that is reaching more and more people may cause thanksgiving to overflow to the glory of God. Therefore we do not lose heart. Though outwardly we are wasting away, yet inwardly we are being renewed day by day.

For our light and momentary troubles are achieving for us an eternal glory that far outweighs them all. So we fix our eyes not on what is seen, but on what is unseen. For what is seen is temporary, but what is unseen is eternal."

So when we are faced with hardships, trials, and temptations:

"Let us fix our eyes on Jesus, the Author and Perfecter of our faith, Who for the joy set before Him endured the cross, scorning its shame, and sat down at the right hand of the throne of God."

"Consider it pure joy, my brothers, whenever you face trials of many kinds, because you know that the testing of your faith develops perseverance. Perseverance must finish its work so that you may be mature and complete, not lacking anything."

Perseverance is a very important part of our Christian experience. We must develop this quality in our lives because without perseverance, our faith will not be able to become refined and perfected.

"Let us not become weary in doing good, for at the proper time we will reap a harvest if we do not give up."

"So do not throw away your confidence; it will be richly rewarded. You need to persevere so that when you have done the will of God, you will receive what He has promised."

The bottom line of your daily walk with Jesus is **"faith expressing itself in love."** No matter how difficult the circumstances seem, you must not stop believing God's Word, and you must not stop living a life of love. You must not be moved away from the promises of God.

There will be times when your faith in God's Word does not seem to be working, but that is the time to persevere rather than quit. When you are mistreated by others, don't stop loving them and don't **"pay back evil for evil, but rather overcome evil with good."**

"Finally, be strong in the Lord and in His mighty power. Put on the full armor of God so that you can take your stand against the devil's schemes. For our struggle is not against flesh and blood, but against the rulers, against the authorities, against the powers of this dark world and against the spiritual forces of evil in the heavenly realms.

Therefore put on the full armor of God, so that when the day of evil comes, you may be able to stand your ground, and after you have done everything, to stand. Stand firm then, with the belt of truth buckled around your waist, with the breastplate of righteousness in place, and with your feet fitted with the readiness that comes from the gospel of peace. In addition to all this, take up the shield of faith, with which you can extinguish all the flaming arrows of the evil one. Take the helmet of salvation and the sword of the Spirit, which is the Word of God. And pray in the Spirit on all occasions with all kinds of prayers and requests. With this in mind, be alert and always keep on praying for all the saints."

Remember "you are now Christ's Ambassador to a lost and dying world. You are also a soldier in God's army. Fight the good fight of faith. If God be for you, who can be against you. Greater is He that is in you, than he that is in the world. You are more than a conqueror through Him who loved you. Take hold of that for which Christ Jesus has taken hold of you. Love your enemies, bless those who persecute you, and pray for those who despitefully use you."

Be a giver. Whatever God has given to you, share it with others who are less fortunate than you. **Freely you have received, therefore freely give. It is more blessed to give than to receive.** When you see someone in need, don't hold back; meet their need in the Name of Jesus.

Jesus is coming soon! While He was still on earth, He said to His followers, **"In my Father's house are many rooms; if it were not so, I would have told you. I am going there to prepare a place for you. And if I go and prepare a place for you, I will come back and take you to be with me that you also may be where I am."**

Since, then, you have been raised with Christ, set your hearts on things above, where Christ is seated at the right hand of God. Set your minds on things above, not on earthly things. For you died, and your life is now hidden with Christ in God. When Christ, Who is your life, appears, then you also will appear with Him in glory.

The Word Of God

God's Written Word, the Bible, is the basis and foundation for this entire book. Everything written in this book is based on Truth as recorded in God's Word. The Bible is God's written record, account, and revelation to mankind of Himself.

There are many portions of Scripture from the Bible used in this book. They appear in **bold faced type** throughout this book. As you reread it, pay special attention to the Words from the Bible, God's Word. Here are some things the Bible says about itself:

"Above all, you must understand that no prophecy of Scripture came about by the prophet's own interpretation. For prophecy never had its origin in the will of man, but men spoke from God as they were carried along by the Holy Spirit."

"From infancy you have known the Holy Scriptures, which are able to make you wise for salvation through faith in Christ Jesus. All Scripture is God-breathed and is useful for teaching, rebuking, correcting and training in righteousness, so that the man of God may be thoroughly equipped for every good work."

The men whom God chose to write and speak the Word of God, were actually carried along by the Holy Spirit, and He breathed His Words right into them. The Bible is the Word of God, not the word of man, and even though God used human instruments to record His Word, It will never pass away. It is Eternal, just as God is Eternal.

"Your Word, O LORD, is Eternal; It stands firm in the Heavens."

"Heaven and earth will pass away, but My Words will never pass away."

"The grass withers and the flowers fall, but the Word of our God stands Forever."

"Every Word of God is flawless; He is a shield to those who take refuge in Him."

"For the Word of God is living and active. Sharper than any double-edged sword, it penetrates even to dividing soul and spirit, joints and marrow; it judges the thoughts and attitudes of the heart."

"For everything that was written in the past was written to teach us, so that through endurance and the encouragement of the Scriptures we might have hope."

The Word of God is the most important thing you can ever read. As you read and study this book, over and over, you will begin building a foundation of Truth from the Scriptures, which are in **Bold text** throughout this book, but we also want to get a copy of the New Testament to you, which is the portion of the Bible that records God's Written Word, beginning with the Birth of Jesus Christ.

This book, "True Happiness Can Be Yours", is not God's Word, even though it contains many quotations from the Bible. We strongly encourage you to write to us for your own copy of the New Testament, which we will send to you free of charge.

You will find an Order Form on the next page. Please complete it and mail it to us. We will mail you a free New Testament, which will help you continue to grow stronger and stronger in Jesus, and get to know Him more and more intimately.

Also on the Order Form, you will find a place to order more copies of this book, free of charge, to give away to family, friends, and people you meet each day. If this book has helped you, it will also help others. This is a tool that you can use to help others know Christ.

The last two pages of this book contains a condensed version of God's Plan of Salvation. This is placed here for you to use to help someone else be reconciled to God by receiving Jesus Christ as their Lord and Savior. The most meaningful times of your Christian life will be when you help other people be restored to a right relationship with their Creator through His Son, Jesus Christ. May you be truly blessed by God as you help others find the True Happiness you have found.

Order Form

Please send me a free New Testament, and _____ free copies of this book, <u>True Happiness Can Be Yours</u>. (Request as many copies as you can use, and we will do our best to supply them.)

Name: _____

Address: _____

_____

City: _____

State/Province: _____

Zip/Postal Code: _____

Country: _____ Age: _____

Cut along the broken lines and mail this Order Form to:

DenSu Ministries, Inc.
P. O. Box 26393
Akron, OH 44319 USA

Or Email Us:
book@densu.com

Visit Our Web Site:
http://www.densu.com

Please use the other side of this Order Form to tell us how you received this book and how it has helped you. Also tell us how and where you plan to use the free copies of this book to help others come to know Christ.

_____

_____

_____

_____

_____

_____

_____

_____

_____

_____

_____

_____

_____

God's Plan Of Salvation

God, the Creator of the Universe, created you with the capacity to be truly happy through an intimate trust relationship with Him. However, you and all mankind went your own way, breaking that trust with God and choosing to live life apart from your Creator.

The devil, Satan, tempted mankind, lying about the character of God, and enticing mankind to distrust God and sin against Him. Sin, unbelief, and disobedience have robbed the human race from the joy, peace, and True Happiness that God intended for every person.

The separation of man from God caused by sin has left people empty, incomplete, and with a void that nothing but God Himself can fill. For centuries, people have tried filling that void with everything the world has to offer, good things and bad things, even religion itself, but they remain empty, fearful, lonely, burdened, and confused.

God never stopped loving mankind who had been created in His own image, but rather made a way, through His Son Jesus Christ, for all mankind to return to Him and His original plan for them.

"For God so loved the world that He gave His one and only Son, that whoever believes in Him shall not perish but have Eternal Life. For God did not send his Son into the world to condemn the world, but to save the world through Him."

Jesus answered, "I am the Way and the Truth and the Life. No one comes to the Father except through Me."

"God made Him (Jesus) Who had no sin to be sin for us, so that in Him we might become the righteousness of God."

"For Christ died for sins once for all, the righteous for the unrighteous, to bring you to God." "For what I received I passed on to you as of first importance: that Christ died for our sins according to the Scriptures, that He was buried, that He was raised on the third day according to the Scriptures."

Jesus Christ died for you so that you can be forgiven for your sins, have a right relationship with God, your Creator, and experience True Happiness, now and forever, through Jesus.

Jesus said, "I am come that they might have life, and that they might have it more abundantly."

Jesus said, "Come to me, all you who are weary and burdened, and I will give you rest. Take my yoke upon you and learn from me, for I am gentle and humble in heart, and you will find rest for your souls."

Jesus said, "I have come into the world as a light, so that no one who believes in Me should stay in darkness."

"For the wages of sin is death, but the gift of God is Eternal Life in Christ Jesus our Lord."

"Yet to all who received Him, to those who believed in His Name, He gave the right to become children of God."

"If you confess with your mouth, "Jesus is Lord," and believe in your heart that God raised Him from the dead, you will be saved."

"Whoever calls on the Name of the Lord will be saved."

You can call on the Name of the Lord right now and receive Jesus Christ as your personal Savior and Lord by praying the following:

Dear God,

I believe that Jesus died for my sins and that You raised Him from the dead. Thank You for giving Your Son for me. Right now, I call upon the Name of Jesus and receive Him into my heart as my Savior and as the Lord of my life.

Thank you, God, for saving me from my sins and for restoring me to a right relationship with You. Help me know You better each day and live a life that is pleasing to You in every way. I want to trust You with every area of my life and obey You. I Love You!

In Jesus's Name, Amen!